WESTERN TIMES BR (W)

ISSUE No.11 - WINTER 2024

Contents

The Transport Treasury

TIMES SERIES

Above: Operating the railway during intense or sustained periods of snow and ice, presented its own unique problems. Complete line blockages necessitating the deployment of snowploughs perhaps being the most spectacular, but equally as debilitating was the effect of ice on point and signal operation. Then there was the battle to keep water columns free running and loco coal in a condition fit for use, before we even consider the small matter of passenger comfort and safety. It seems highly appropriate to take a closer look at these challenges in this Winter Issue of *Western Times.* You can almost feel the chill in this view looking north at Princes Risborough as a 'Large Prairie' departs with a service to Oxford, the final week of passenger operation on that line in January 1963.   *Doug Nicholls.*

Front Cover: The shed cleaners at Exeter have done a respectable job in maintaining the shine on the mixed traffic lined black paintwork of No. 5959 *Mawley Hall.* The 4-6-0 was only resident at 83C for a short period between December 1956 and March 1957, so this photograph was taken between those dates. The locomotive went into lined green livery following a Heavy General in February 1958 and was withdrawn from Tyseley shed in September 1962 having run some 1,069,787 miles.   *R C Riley (RCRC 4188).*

Rear Cover: The platform at Kingsbridge looks an absolute picture on 15 July 1958. The station staff have literally filled the flower borders with Pink Carnations, Geraniums and Begonias in order to brighten the day of travellers to the South Devon terminus. The original GWR running-in board and a well stocked goods yard and carriage sidings complete the idyllic scene. This popular branch line through the South Hams district will be the subject of an upcoming article within these pages next year.   *R C Riley (RCRC 3520).*

© The Transport Treasury 2024.

ISBN 978-1-913251-785-7

First Published in 2024 by Transport Treasury Publishing Ltd.
16 Highworth Close, High Wycombe, HP13 7PJ.

Compiled and designed in the UK. Printed in Tarxien, Malta by Gutenberg Press Ltd.

The copyright holders hereby give notice that all rights to this work are reserved.
Aside from brief passages for the purpose of review, no part of this work may be reproduced,
copied by electronic or other means, or otherwise stored in any information storage and
retrieval system without written permission from the Publisher.

This includes the illustrations herein which shall remain the copyright of the respective copyright holder.
Every effort has been made to identify and credit photographers where known.

INTRODUCTION

The adage goes that 'A Picture Paints a Thousand Words', and that sentiment certainly applies to those of us interested in railway history and the associated research and modelling activities. Where would we be without that 'definitive' piece of visual evidence to prove or dispel uncertain information, or to illuminate that vital element of missing detail? In our field of interest, we are blessed that a large number of dedicated individuals have recorded the diversity of life on the railway with their cameras, over many years. Without this rich resource, captured by professional and amateur photographers alike, the task of documenting and ultimately enjoying our hobby would be much the poorer as a result.

Imagery plays an integral part in all aspects of a publication like *Western Times* and the editorial team are blessed in having unlimited access to the huge archive curated by The Transport Treasury. Of equal importance is the myriad of photographs that surface from private collections, many of which have not seen the light of day before and never fail to delight. Take the images supplied by Alan Postlethwaite to support his Welsh Marches article in this issue as a case in point. You really have to wonder what is still out there, yet to be discovered in private collections or hidden away at the back of shelves in the more established archives. Unearthing absolute gems never fails to surprise, a recent example of which is the stunning photograph of 'Dean Single' No. 3003 *Avalanche* reproduced on pages 60-61.

Then we come to the process of how this imagery is copied and presented, which often divides opinion. Wherever possible your editor will utilise High Resolution (300dpi) digital files for both colour and black and white images, which will be sized according to where they sit within the final page layout. These digital files will have been scanned from the original negatives, slides or prints to include the whole frame area, so as to not lose that essential piece of information at the extreme edges. This policy of maintaining the integrity of the original is fundamental and any manipulation will only follow basic 'darkroom' style techniques of exposure, contrast and colour balance optimisation. Cloning is not advocated, other than the removal of dust marks and scratches, and cropping will only remove surplus areas of sky or landscape that offers no specific value to the composition. On occasions, purely for aesthetic or historical reasons, the sepia or age toning of an original photograph will be retained, but the digital addition of filters or colourisation is not undertaken. The ethic and value of colourising older archive material is an argument we will save for another day! One final comment relates to the editorial decision to occasionally use images that do not meet the normal expected standards of quality. This compromise will only be considered if the content is of such important or rare value, that no better alternative is available. Latitude sometimes has to be given for a photographer's expertise, or the limitations of early equipment and film stock. This material does often have its place though.

We fully understand the inexhaustible thirst for new photographs, or variations that show a specific subject or location on a particular date. We all have our preferences and areas of interest, and we will always attempt to vary the output to cater for a broad church. However, sometimes people's expectations need to be realistic. It is entirely possible that some things were never recorded in the first place, or if it was, that the evidence hasn't survived the passage of time. We can only guess at, and lament, the quantity of photographic material that has been inadvertently disposed of over the years, due to a lack of understanding as to its historical value or to inadequate preservation measures. To conclude on a positive tone, we must also be thankful for those unexpected photographic treasures that are still regularly unearthed, and which it is our absolute pleasure to present to you, the readership.

It is with deep sadness that we must report the sudden death of **Brian Wheeler**, former railwayman and contributor to *Western Times*. We know he took pride and enjoyment in seeing his words and experiences brought to print in his articles recalling his time as a BR(W) Apprentice and detailing his many footplate adventures. These accounts from those who actually 'did it' rather than watch it being done by someone else are extremely valuable, and Brian's passing only strengthens our resolve to bring these stories to the collective. Our sincere condolences go out to his family and friends.

--- o O o---

Editor: Andrew Malthouse

Editorial Assistant: Jeremy Clements

To contact the editorial team please email: **WesternTimes@mail.com**

For sales, subscriptions and back issues of *Western Times* please go to: **www.ttpublishing.co.uk**

DISCOVERING THE WELSH MARCHES
ALAN POSTLETHWAITE

This article covers two photographic expeditions that I made in 1962 while undergoing industrial training with English Electric in Stafford. On two glorious Bank Holiday weekends, I took my bike on the train to Shrewsbury and then pedalled furiously in search of steam. On the Welsh side of the border, I found steam around Llanymynech, Four Crosses and Llanfyllin. On the English side, starting at Shrewsbury, I rode west to Hanwood and south to Craven Arms. I also paid brief visits to the Shropshire & Montgomery line, the Minsterley branch, the Bishop's Castle branch and the Welshpool & Llanfair railway. It was a labour of love to capture 'the train in the countryside'. All was new to me, having grown up on the Southern. What I discovered was a heavenly countryside of verdant valleys, enticing foothills and friendly people everywhere.

The Cambrian Railways was an amalgamation in 1864 of twelve smaller railways covering mid-Wales and the west coast. The oldest of these ran from Three Cocks to Talyllyn Junction, part of the horse-drawn Hay Railway that opened in 1816. Most relevant to this article is the Oswestry and Newtown Railway that opened in 1860-61. It followed the border with England from the Severn almost to the Dee. Its headquarters and workshops were at Oswestry in Shropshire. The Cambrian connected with the GWR at Oswestry and with the LNWR at Whitchurch.

The Shrewsbury and Welshpool Railway opened to Minsterley in 1861 and to Welshpool in 1862. It was worked originally by the LNWR over which the GWR had running powers. In 1865, the two companies became joint owners. This line is the only connection remaining between the Cambrian and the rest of Britain's railway network. In pre-car-ownership days, holidaymakers used this route to multiple resorts on the Irish Sea including Butlins Holiday Camp at Pwllheli. It still provides access to many of the Great Little Trains of Wales, all narrow gauge.

The line from Shrewsbury to Craven Arms opened in 1852, jointly owned by the LNWR and GWR. It reached Hereford the following year. The Heart of Wales line from Craven Arms was built by the LNWR as far as Llandovery. It then made junctions with other railways to serve South and South West Wales. Details of the smaller lines in this article are given in the relevant captions. The Cambrian Railways amalgamated with the Great Western in 1922. The northern section from Welshpool to Oswestry closed in 1965 under the Beeching axe together with the Llanfyllin branch.

Please enjoy this excursion along the Welsh borders during the late Steam Age. All photographs were captured by the author unless credited and are now copyrighted to the Bluebell Railway Archives.

Above: In a scene that typifies the bucolic nature of the countryside of the Welsh Marches, Ivatt 2-6-0 No. 46509 nears Bryngwyn in the verdant Llanfyllin valley. The LMS-designed 2MT Mogul was built in 1952 at Swindon, and was on the books of the Western Region until transfer to the London Midland in early 1965. At the time of this 1962 photograph, it was allocated to Oswestry (89D).

The Welsh Marches

There is no precise geographical line on a map that defines the extent of the area known as the Welsh Marches. The term 'March' originates from the 13th-century Middle Ages word *marche*, meaning a border region or frontier. In this case it relates to the lands between England and the Principality of Wales, particularly the counties of Shropshire, Herefordshire, Montgomeryshire and Radnorshire (now Powys).

These feudal lands had been the seat of much historical division, but were united by the routes of the Cambrian Railway, Shrewsbury & Hereford Railway, Shrewsbury & Welshpool Railway and the Potteries, Shrewsbury & North Wales Railway (The Potts). Later absorbed into the Great Western Railway empire, with London & North Western Railway running rights over some routes, these railways ran through beautiful pastoral scenery connecting small towns and picturesque villages and forever retained a unique rural charm.

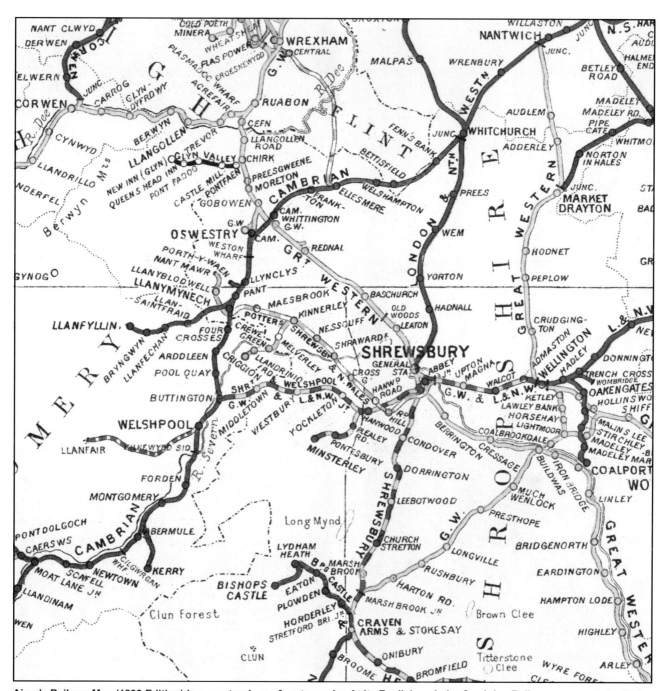

Airey's Railway Map (1893 Edition) is a masterpiece of cartography. At its English end, the Cambrian Railways connected with the GWR, LNWR and 'The Potts'. The Cambrian main line remains open to this day from the west coast as far as Welshpool, then cutting across to Shrewsbury. The Heart of Wales line also remains open, running from Shrewsbury through Craven Arms to Llanelli.

Above: The Montgomeryshire market town of Llanfyllin once had a fine station, straight as a die, seen here in the early morning.

Below: No. 46509 has arrived at the terminus at Llanfyllin with the 'B-set' branch service on Whitsun 1962. The porter has deposited the contents of E147 No. W6776W onto the cart for onward despatch, and the loco will shortly run round its train ready for the return journey.

2nd-SINGLE SINGLE-2nd
7922   7922

Llanfyllin to
Llanfyllin
Bryngwyn   Llanfyllin
Bryngwyn
BRYNGWYN
(W) 4d.   Fare   4d.   (W)
For conditions see over For conditions see over

Above: Having now completed the run round manoeuvre and re-coupled to the 'B-set', No. 46509 awaits a return to Oswestry. The terminus at Llanfyllin had a sizeable red brick station building, goods shed and neat signal cabin. The loading dock to the left stabling the pair of 16T mineral wagons, often hosted an obligatory 'Camping Coach' during Great Western Railway days and for a short period following Nationalisation.

Above: Finally, No. 46509 departs Llanfyllin with the late afternoon train, framed by the telegraph pole and water tower. The Cambrian vintage platform starter signal can just be discerned to the right of the signal cabin, as can the distant tower of St Myllin's Church within the village. The concrete in the centre foreground marks the site of the former engine shed, which closed in 1952.

Above: Another Swindon-built Ivatt 2-6-0, this time No. 46519, arrives at Llanfyllin with the modest daily freight working. This locomotive emerged from 'A' Shop in February 1953 as part of Lot.394. It spent its first ten years allocated to Oswestry, before moving to Machynlleth, Shrewsbury, Nuneaton and Stoke. Withdrawal came in October 1966 and scrapping at Cohens yard in Kettering, after a working life of less than 14 years.

The signal box is of a Dutton & Co. design and contained a 12-lever frame.

Right: Following a short period of shunting at the terminus, the train departs back towards Oswestry. A solitary 12T van and 'Toad' hardly seem economical fare for a tender engine and a crew of three railwaymen. The whole scene is indicative of the decline of the rural railway network of the early 1960s. That said, you still have to admire the immaculate state of the permanent way.

The Llanfyllin branch of the Cambrian opened on 10 April 1863, and was closed under the Beeching axe on 18 January 1965, as was the main line through Llanymynech.

Top: The first halt out from Llanfyllin on the return down the branch to Llanymynech was Bryngwyn, seen here in all its tranquil rural glory. It featured a basic wooden platform with a corrugated metal shelter and two patterns of oil lamp and served the villages of Bwlch-y-cibau and Brynderwen. Originally named Brongwyn Halt, it was renamed after the nearby Bryngwyn Hall in 1923.

Right: The next intermediate station at Llanfechain was beautified by an imposing Scots Pine tree and a bank of spring flowers. The neat red brick station building, stone road bridge and grassy cattlepen add to the scene. The building survives today as a private residence, albeit with the addition of an extension to the far elevation.

The issuing of single tickets from Llansantffraid to Llanfechain Halt (a distance of only 1½ miles) must have been a relatively rare occurance!

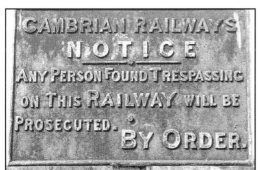

Above: Various relics from the previous ownership survived along the Llanfyllin branch, including this Cambrian Railway trespass notice. The author of course obeyed its instruction to the letter!

Above: The rudimentary Carreghofa Halt was a late addition to the branch. It was opened by the GWR in 1938 on a new spur that joined the former Nantmawr branch (closed in 1925) and enabled Llanfyllin trains to enter Llanymynech station from the south.

Right: Ivatt Mogul No. 46509 departs Carreghofa Halt beneath the Montgomery Canal. Just about here was once the junction for the original 'Potts' line to the Nantmawr quarries.

The Potteries, Shrewsbury & North Wales Railway ran from the Flintshire quarries to Shrewsbury, but was never extended to the Potteries as planned. Known as 'The Potts', it opened in 1866 but was unprofitable, closing in 1880 (apart from the Nantmawr branch). In 1907, the line was taken over by Colonel Stephens and renamed the Shropshire & Montgomeryshire Light Railway. The new line opened in 1911 followed by the Criggion branch a year later. The bridge over the River Severn at Melverley was declared unsafe in 1932 and all passenger services ceased a year later. In 1941, the line was taken over by the War Department and used for the storage of ammunition. The line finally closed in 1960, except for the northern part of the Nantmawr branch which survived until around 1979.

Below: More signage, this time of Great Western Railway origin. The language and justification for such a notice must be admired.

Above: Llanymynech was a junction station for both the Llanfyllin branch and 'The Potts' through to Shrewsbury. This view looking north, is dominated by the impressive Cambrian Railway footbridge, with to the far right the 'Potts' platform served by a humble wooden shelter. This line had operated as the Shropshire & Montgomeryshire Light Railway between 1911 and 1960, and whilst the track was quickly lifted following closure, the yard at Llanymynech was retained for wagon storage for a number of years after.

Below: Map showing the extent of the Potteries, Shrewsbury & North Wales (later the S&MLR).   *Welsh Railways Research Circle.*

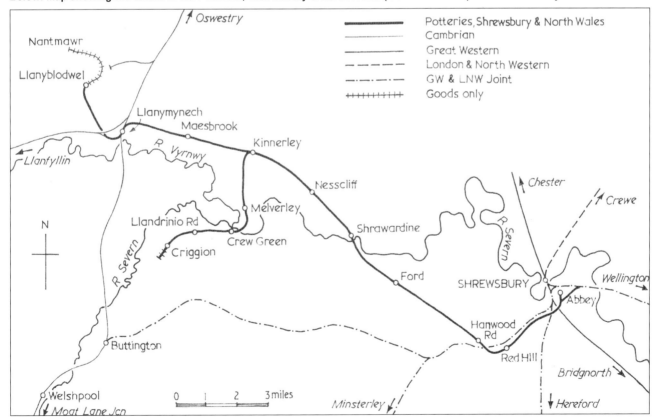

Above: Ford and Crossgates was half way between Llanymynech and Shrewsbury. It sported a stone platform, a wooden building and a van body for storage. The white board is a mystery, unlikely to be a signal sighting shield and possibly of War Department origin.

Below: 'The Potts' ran parallel with the GWR-LNWR joint line out of Shrewsbury as far as Meole Brace halt, located beneath the A5 road bridge. The halt opened in 1911 and closed in 1933. Twenty nine years later, its rotting remains are still discernible as a halt, serving as a memorial to Colonel Stephens and his empire of nation-wide light railways, all built at minimal cost.

Above: Returning to the section of Cambrian mainline between Llanymynech and Buttington Junction, we find Churchward Mogul No. 7313 departing Llanymynech heading south towards Welshpool, passing the divergence of the Llanfyllin branch, which is obscured behind the train. The engine was a resident of Croes Newydd shed and was a matter of weeks away from being withdrawn.

Bottom: Four Crosses was the first station south of Llanymynech, and appears immaculately kept in this view. It had a neat arrangement of staggered platforms, from which a two-coach southbound train can be seen departing. The brick-built station building and goods shed were substantial structures and the signal box is of 1896 vintage. A private siding was provided to serve an adjacent Creamery and the station is probably best remembered for its mention in the 1964 song 'Slow Train' by Flanders and Swann.

Top: Moving now to the LNWR/GWR Joint line (the North & West route) and the sad site of Condover station looking south. Built by the Shrewsbury and Hereford Railway and opened in 1852, the station closed in 1958, although the signal box still remained active.

Middle: Further south near Dorrington, Newton Abbot 'Warship' No. D828 *Magnificent* heads the 1V93 09.10am Liverpool-Plymouth, which it would have taken over at Crewe.

Bottom: No. 6928 *Underley Hall* of Pontypool Road shed (86G) heads a Class C express fitted van train past the goods loops at Dorrington.

Above: As can be seen from this view at Dorrington looking north towards Shrewsbury, the former station buildings were substantial. It closed to passenger services on 9 June 1958, and in the customary manner the platform faces have been removed from both sides for safety reasons. Like at Condover, the signals and signal box were of GWR pattern.

By the time of this 19 August 1962 visit, there was some evidence of general goods in the yard but the principal remaining freight was milk tankers and vans serving the nearby large dairy facility. All remaining goods traffic was withdrawn on 3 May 1965, and thus another rural Shropshire wayside station was consigned to the history books.

Right: As was the case at Condover, the signal box at Dorrington remained operational. I was invited into the cabin by signalman E.H. Marsh of Church Stretton. As was the norm for the time, he was immaculately turned out, as was his box.

The rear catch handles and front-mounted lever leads were a common pattern for the GWR and other UK railways. The black and white chevrons were for a detonator lever (arrow pointing downwards denoted the 'Down Line' dets). There was also a hand generator for a remote facing point, the limit of hand operation being 350 yards.

2nd. SPECIAL
CHEAP DAY

Craven Arms
& Stokesay

to

CHURCH STRETTON
(W)

For conditions see over

SPECIAL
CHEAP DAY 2nd

Church Stretton

to

CRAVEN ARMS
& Stokesay

(W)

For conditions see over

3359

3359

Above: 'Warship' No. D845 *Sprightly* slows to a halt at Craven Arms with an express bound for the West Country. This class member was instantly recognisable due to its unique livery featuring a reduced size warning panel and white cab-roof brow, which it carried between August 1961 and October 1963. The station was beautified by variegated paving, a botanic platform and intricate canopy trelliswork, making it a delight to alight.

Below: Looking south from the opposite platform, a Class 120 Swindon Cross-Country DMU departs signalled towards Hereford. The ex-LNWR 'Central Wales' line to Knighton can just be seen diverging to the right beyond the signal box.

Right: The magnificent chocolate and cream enamel running in board must lay claim to having the most characters of any on the BR(W).

Named after a 17th century Coaching Inn, the town of Craven Arms expanded following the arrival of the Shrewsbury & Hereford Railway on 21 April 1852. Craven Arms and Stokesay became an important five-way junction station with services to South Wales (LNWR), Hereford (Joint), Wellington via Much Wenlock (GWR), Shrewsbury (Joint) and Bishop's Castle (Independent). In a much curtailed form it remains open.

Above: Unsurprisingly such an important junction justified an engine shed, this stone four-road slate hipped-roof structure was built by the LNWR and opened in 1869. Including a turntable and coaling stage, all on the west side of the line north of the station, it became a sub-shed of Shrewsbury. It played host to an eclectic mix of ex-LMS and GWR locomotives from small passenger tanks to heavy freight types, as typified here on 19 August 1962 by Stanier 8F 2-8-0 No. 48732 and Collett Goods 0-6-0 No.3205 (now preserved). The shed was closed on 22 May 1964, although the structure survived into the 1970s before final demolition.

Left: The Bishop's Castle Railway was an independent line that opened in 1865 and closed in 1935 following heavy losses and eventual bankruptcy. The original ambition to reach Montgomery in Wales was never realised, resulting in the unusual reversal of trains at Lydham Heath in order to reach the terminus at Bishop's Castle.

Diverging from the main line to the north of Craven Arms at Stretford Bridge Junction, it ran westwards for just over ten miles serving rural Shropshire villages and the border town after which it was named.

Twenty seven years after closure, the course of the trackbed was just about discernible near Horderley.

Above: Our journey around the Welsh Marches moves to the section of LNWR/GWR Joint line between Shrewsbury and Welshpool. Standard Class 3MT 2-6-2T No. 82005 is seen heading a stopping service through what can only be described as the most immaculate of shallow cuttings near to Hanwood. The May 1952 Swindon built locomotive was a resident of Machynlleth (89C) at this time.

Below: Shrewsbury allocated Churchward 2-6-0 No. 7329 heads the ten-coach Up 'Cambrian Coast Express' (1A70) on the section of line just east of Hanwood station. It will be relieved by a larger 4-6-0 upon arrival at Shrewsbury, where the train will reverse before continuing its journey south towards Birmingham. The over-bridge carrying the former 'Potts' line was just behind the photographer.

Above: The Shrewsbury and Welshpool Railway was joint GWR-LNWR, opening in 1861. Hanwood, the first station out of Shrewsbury, was the junction for the Minsterley branch, served by the line on the left. The signal box is an extended Saxby & Stevens (Type 1).

Below: At various locations during my trip around the Welsh Marches, I sketched the details into a trusty field-notebook. This reproduced example shows the station and immediate environs at Hanwood, now absolute research gold for the railway modeller!

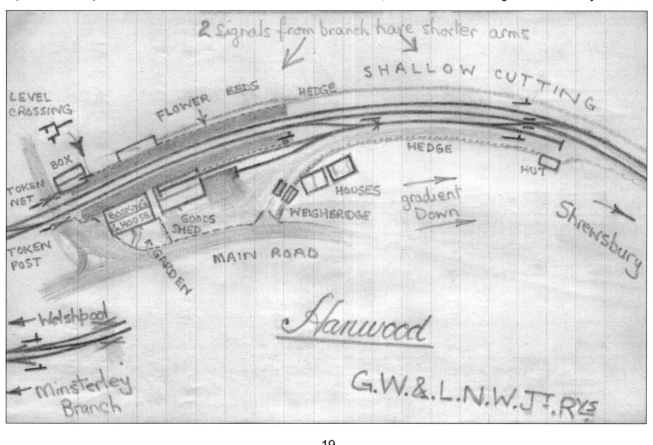

Above: Minsterley station was the terminus of a 6½ mile branch from Cruckmeole Junction west of Hanwood. Opened in 1861, it became the truncated result of a joint LNWR/GWR plan to join the Cambrian main line at Montgomery. Although passenger traffic ceased in 1951, the branch remained open to goods until 1967, primarily serving the Minsterley Creamery. In the somewhat neglected state of its later years, a handful of wagons occupy the yard, whilst a black cat stands guard on the redundant platform.

Above: The large station at Welshpool was one of the most important on the Cambrian main line and consisted of three through platforms and a bay in the Up direction. The imposing main building with its huge canopy, was built in a French renaissance style and opened in 1860. The 2' 6" gauge Welshpool & Llanfair Railway had exchange sidings in the goods yard behind the footbridge.

Above: Welshpool & Llanfair Railway Beyer Peacock 0-6-0 No. 822 is recorded negotiating Seven Stars level crossing with a mixed goods train. Opening in 1903 and originally operated by the Cambrian Railway, the 9-mile line closed to passengers in 1931 and to all traffic in November 1956. *John J Smith*.

Right: An early preservation scene captures *The Earl* near Castle Caereinion.

Above: The railway was originally operated by a pair of compact 0-6-0T locomotives delivered from Beyer Peacock in 1903, No.1 *The Earl* and No. 2 *Countess* (renumbered 822 and 823 respectively by the GWR in 1923). The line was resurrected in 1962, although curtailed at Raven Square at the Welshpool end. At Llanfair Caereinion *The Earl* is seen from afar at the start my long cycle ride home.

TENDER FIRST IN THE PROVINCES
FROM THE ARCHIVES OF R C RILEY

In planning a range of standard steam classes by the recently-formed British Railways, much effort was devoted to ensuring cab comfort, so far as the traditional configuration of a tender locomotive would permit. Western crews were reportedly ambivalent concerning the new motive power although men at Canton embraced their Britannias more enthusiastically than colleagues at other depots. Elsewhere in the Principality, Ivatt Class 2 moguls (as witnessed in the previous article) and their closely related BR-designed fellows were well received. Apart from ease of servicing afforded by excellent accessibility, crews who had been brought up on a diet of Dean Goods with their 2500- or 3000-gallon tenders appreciated the more enclosed cabs. The footplate of an ageing Dean on a warm summer day would have been a pleasant place of work but it was a different matter amid rain or snow served up among the Welsh hills in other seasons.

Apart from controls and revised lookout disciplines, reverse running with tank engines fitted with overall cabs presented no major difficulties although older open-backed cabs were uncomfortable during adverse weather. Equally, smaller tenders provided little protection to the rear so reverse running was usually only over shorter distances or under special circumstances.

Above: On Sunday, 23 September 1951 No. 6929 *Whorlton Hall* (a long term resident of Banbury) accompanied by a Toad of non-GWR origin was near Brill north of Ashendon Junction, presumably on its way to pick up a train. The headlamp code denotes a Class J Train (through mineral or empty wagon train) although a Class G code with single lamp placed centrally immediately above the buffer beam might be equally appropriate (Light engine or with one or two brake vans attached). The 1941 built locomotive carries the mixed traffic lined black livery, and note also that the tender water filler lid has been left open after the last replenishment. *(RCR 3457).*

Tyseley's No. 5369 (Head lamp Code J – Mineral or empty wagon train) is approaching the camera light engine near Stratford-upon-Avon on Monday, 16 April 1956. This locomotive survived until November 1963, one of the last of the 53xx-series at work. *(RCR 5872)*.

Newton Abbot-allocated No. 70022 *Tornado* is heading towards Aller Junction with a passenger service, passing No. 5071 *Spitfire* (also 83A) on Wednesday 13 July 1955. The Castle's head lamp code indicates a light engine although the train looks like an empty stock working from the Kingswear branch. The date was prior to the installation of the turntable at Goodrington, so a quick run-round at either Paignton or Kingswear and a return working with the locomotive in reverse to Newton would have been the quickest means of easing congestion on this busy summer route. The 'Brit' left 83A for Canton the following December as part of the concentration of WR's allocation at the Welsh depot. *(RCR 6462)*.

Class '2251' No. 3219 of Reading depot is found working close to home at Southcote Junction, as it takes the freight-only Coley Branch on Friday 20 April 1956. This locomotive was a minor celebrity as the last GWR-design 0-6-0 to enter service and one of only two of that wheel arrangement delivered by British Railways. *(RCR 7122).*

Many of the Riley images reveal long lost features of the railway as in this example. Behind the locomotive to the left and right is a rake of cattle wagons standing in front of Reading Goods Line West Box which opened with 43 levers circa 1896 and closed 7 February 1965. On Saturday, 29 September 1956, Truro's No. 1022 *County of Northampton* was reversing off Reading shed. This class was popular in Cornwall and as the engine was facing west, its next duty was probably to take over from foreign motive power on a service bound for Plymouth, or into the Duchy. *(RCR 8009).*

Above: Locally-allocated No. 5032 *Usk Castle* was departing Newton Abbot tender-first with the 7.40am Saturdays only Paddington-Paignton (TRN 117) on 19 July 1958. This train had paused on the through line indicating a stop unscheduled in the public timetable, made specifically to change motive power. The time taken with this manoeuvre was probably of little consequence as by then delays would be accumulating on this busy day. The Castle was therefore facing the right way to work a later Up service. The unidentified Hall standing at the entrance to the lower shed yard carries TRN 535 (1.40 pm Saturdays only Kingswear-Paddington) so presumably it is waiting to visit NA's turntable before a run down the branch in reverse to work its allotted Up service. *(RCR 12364)*.

Below: February 1921 built Churchward 2-6-0 No. 6320 of Westbury shed (82D), is recorded working a permanent way train at Dauntsey on Sunday 6 November 1960. This locomotive was the only mogul and the smallest participant in the oil-burner programme. It was so equipped between March 1947 and August 1949 and was apparently entirely satisfactory in that condition. *(RCR 15473)*.

An occasional attraction of the Riley portfolio was Dick's efforts to record the same train or locomotive through a sequence of movements. On Sunday 7 July 1957, he captured No. 6019 *King Henry V* of Old Oak Common passing Lipson Junction, the western point of the triangle that enclosed Laira shed (Insert Right). A little later that day, he photographed the same engine reversing past what he cryptically described as 'Laira Station' on its way to the depot. This was actually the remains of Laira Halt, served by the Millbay-Plympton steam rail motor service until closure due to road competition in 1930. The practice of changing the locomotive on express services at North Road station meant that there was much light engine tender-first running between there and Laira. The depot was built on a quite constricted site that had previously been occupied by a large pond and a sewage works. Had Churchward chosen the other possible location at Tavistock Junction, light engine movements would have been an even greater operational impediment to an already busy stretch of main line.

(RCR 10984 & 10986).

Above: No. 6916 *Misterton Hall* (89A Shrewsbury) reversing through Mutley, Plymouth having come off Laira depot and is bound for North Road on Saturday 8 July 1961. That year saw revision of the TRN system on alpha-numeric principles but confusingly the 'M74' chalked on the smokebox door related to a Cardiff-Crewe/ Liverpool service, likely one of the locomotive's recent turns . Built in June 1941, this locomotive was the first of the wartime production Halls to enter service unnamed, except for 'HALL CLASS' in painted plain letters on the centre splasher face. It was properly christened in April 1946.   *(RCR 16033).*

Below: Collett Goods 0-6-0 No. 2289 is seen approaching Banbury yard on Saturday 27 April 1963 with a Class J through mineral or empty wagon train. This engine was withdrawn in May 1964 from Banbury shed, by then re-coded from 84C to 2D.   *(RCR 16965).*

Above: As the tender to tank engine transformation of Class 119 involved modification only above the running plate, the distinctive style of double frames was retained with sandwich outside and plate inside, a combination described as 'practically indestructible'. Comparison with the image on the opposite page reveals that the front sandboxes remain of the tall variety but slightly narrower while the typical tool box has been mounted between the centre and rear splashers. No. 123, which was recorded at Newport Dock Street on an unknown date, carried a Wolverhampton Type W3 boiler on conversion in December 1879, followed by an S4 from June 1901. Records indicate that a B4 boiler was fitted in July 1920 and pannier tanks the following October before reverting to another S4 boiler in January 1924. Absence of a date for the image plus the camera angle prevents determination of the boiler type in this view. Withdrawal took place in November 1927. *Courtesy of the Stephenson Locomotive Society.*

Below: There is no recorded date or location for this image of No. 120 which acquired a B4 boiler and pannier tanks in March 1917. It remained in this condition until withdrawal in September 1933 as the last in service. In spite of the strong construction, quite sturdy tie bars have been fitted to the outside frames which is perhaps excusable given that they enjoyed a working career of 72 years. *Courtesy of the Stephenson Locomotive Society.*

THE PANNIER STORY
PART 3 - WOLVERHAMPTON REBUILDS & SMALL LOCOMOTIVES

Production of the remaining 0-6-0STs by the works at Wolverhampton comprised two distinct forms. Commencing in 1878, seventeen were created by rebuild of a like number of 0-6-0s that had been constructed elsewhere and which generally conformed in size, weight and power output with the classes described in Part 2.

The second category related to the 310 small 0-6-0STs produced between 1874 and 1905. This fleet comprised 308 locomotives that were new builds plus two that were reconstructions of early machines. They formed a Wolverhampton 'trademark design' exclusively associated with the works; a modern version did eventually emanate from Swindon but only after the company had been nationalised.

The Rebuilds

The purpose behind the creation of 17 large type 0-6-0STs, through addition of tanks and bunkers, is obscure. The donor 0-6-0s came from two capable classes designed for goods work and the programme seems strange considering the extensive construction of new, large type 0-6-0STs around this time.

Class 119

Before the northern workshops were sufficiently developed to undertake such work, twelve examples of 0-6-0 Class 57 were built at Swindon (1855/6 as 1st Goods Lot) followed by twenty-four of 0-6-0 Class 79:

Loco Nos.	Works Nos.	Lot Nos.	Year
79-84	13-18	2nd Goods	1857
85-90	19-24	3rd Goods	1857/ 8
119-124	27-32	4th Goods	1861
125-130	33-38	5th Goods	1862

The later type differed from Class 57 in a 6" reduction in wheel diameter to 4' 6", increased over the years to 4' 7½" by use of thicker tyres. Together with cylinder dimensions increased from 15½" x 22" to 16" x 24" and boiler pressure raised from 120 to 140 lb/ sq in, these changes yielded a 50% increase in tractive effort over Class 57. Except for the fitting of 17" diameter cylinders to Nos. 83, 90, 119, 120, 123-30, Class 79 remained largely unaltered in their early years. These changes could be easily accommodated through retention of

the original chassis form which comprised outside sandwich and inside plate frames, an immensely strong combination.

After roughly 20 years' service, all 24 (tender) locomotives which had been built with Type R6 boilers (three rings, dome over raised firebox) were subjected to renewal. Between March 1877 and July 1880 all of the first two lots plus No. 122 had replacement boilers fitted. All received Type W3 boilers (three rings, centre dome, flush firebox) except for the last renewal, that of No. 85 which received the then modern Swindon-designed Type S3 (three rings, centre dome, flush firebox) in July 1880. The seven processed in 1877 included No. 122 in August which probably accounts for its exclusion from the later renewal exercise.

The second stage was more comprehensive and addressed all of 4th and 5th Goods Lots except for No. 122. This programme involved installation of Type W3 boilers as were currently being fitting on all but one of the 2nd and 3rd Lots. It is believed that the entire class (i.e. tender and tank versions) were renewed in the 1877-83 period at Wolverhampton although the fitting of a Type S3 boiler to 0-6-0 No. 85 suggested that this case may have been carried out at Swindon.

Later boiler changes followed the usual irregular pattern with some significant intervals between installation of Belpaire boilers and fitting of pannier tanks. As discussed earlier, if the two tasks were effected during the same workshops visit then unduly long periods out

Above: Daniel Gooch's second standard gauge 0-6-0 design with 4' 6" driving wheels was built at Swindon in the period 1857-62 under Goods Lots Nos. 2nd to 5th. This rather poor quality image shows 0-6-0 No. 122 with an S2 type boiler which it acquired in February 1892. This was the only member of the 119-130 number series to remain a tender locomotive.

of service must have resulted. However, it was uncharacteristic for the chronological and numerical order of saddle tank conversions to coincide. No reference can traced where this phenomenon has been remarked upon before and it is surmised that probably changes in locomotive identity were effected as the exercise progressed.

Built in 1861, withdrawal of No. 120 after 72 years, demonstrated the sturdiness of the original construction. Career life-span was sustained by contemporary recognition that a significant element of mainline traffic demand could be handled by tank locomotives. The durability of the sandwich/ inside plate frame structure bequeathed to Class 119 from its 0-6-0 Class 79 predecessor was amply proven by this longevity.

The relationship between six-wheeled, six-coupled tender and tank locomotives will be explored later in the context of total fleet deployment and traffic operating patterns. Nevertheless, the tender to tank conversion resulted in extended careers:

Class	79	79/119
Running Nos.	79-90/ 122	119-21/ 23-30
Average in years :-		
As **0-6-0**	56	19
As **0-6-0ST/PT**	n/a	44

The conversion dates to 0-6-0ST Class 119 and all recorded subsequent boiler changes are listed below:

Loco No.	Built Swindon R6 Boiler	Rebuilt 0-6-0ST W3 Boiler	Later Boiler Changes	Pannier Conversion	Withdrawn
119	Dec-61	Dec-78	S4 Jun-95	n/a	Apr-19
120	Dec-61	May-79	S4 Jun-95/ B4 Feb-17	Mar-17	Sep-33
121	Dec-61	Oct-79	S4 Jun-97/ S2 Feb-06/ S4 Mar-09/ B4 Dec-17/ B4a Jan-26	Apr-18	Sep-28
123	Dec-61	Dec-79	S4 Jun-01/ B4 Jul-20/ S4 Jan-24	Oct-20	Nov-27
124	Dec-61	Apr-80	R3 Nov-05/ S4 Mar-03/ B4 Jan-17	Mar-17	May-27
125	May-62	Jul-80	S4 Jul-98/ B4 Apr-16	Jul-16	Jan-26
126	May-62	Mar-81	S4 Dec-98/ B4 Sep-20	Oct-20	Jul-28
127	May-62	Aug-81	S4 Jul-97	n/a	Nov-10
128	Jun-62	May-82	S4 Apr-99/ R3 Jan-10/ S4 Dec-13	Dec-23	Jan-27
129	Jul-62	Jul-82	S4 May-97/ B4 Aug-13	Apr-13	May-19
130	Jul-62	Feb-83	S4 Dec-99/ B4 Sep-13	Dec-13	May-19

Above: Class 322 built 1864/5 has been rated as the best of all 0-6-0s owned by the GWR which makes rebuild (1878-85) of six 'Beyers' as 0-6-0STs appear counter-intuitive. No. 325, seen here at Stafford Road on an unknown date had been converted from an 0-6-0 No. 337 in March 1880. It probably acquired a B4 boiler and pannier tanks in August 1918, although for unexplained reasons the official date was October 1920. The tool boxes have been mounted either side of the bunker and the rear sandboxes are awkwardly located. These engines must have been less comfortable for crews than the tender version. *Courtesy of the Stephenson Locomotive Society.*

Class 322

The newly formed Beyer Peacock & Co. supplied eight NG 2-2-2s (Works Nos 1-4/ 15-18) in 1855/6 to a design instigated by Daniel Gooch which closely followed broad gauge construction principles. Such was Beyer's progress and reputation for build quality that by 1864, Gooch was content to leave design and construction of the 30 members of double-framed Class 322 (328) entirely in the maker's hands. These highly regarded locomotives were the last six-coupled machines supplied by a contractor to the GWR until 1928 when Armstrong-Whitworth delivered 0-6-2T Class 56xx Nos. 6650-99.

It is reported that it had originally been intended to rebuild all 30 Beyers as 0-6-0STs and apparently the original numbers would be retained by the tank version. This would have formed a continuation of the programme that had commenced in December 1878 with Class 79 No. 119 as the first 0-6-0/ 0-6-0ST conversion. Between 1878 and 1885 six of the Beyers were rebuilt at Wolverhampton as 0-6-0STs following

Above: Beyer Class 322 0-6-0 No. 354 was in final condition with a B4 boiler when photographed at Leamington MPD on an unrecorded date. This locomotive carried this boiler type from May 1901 until withdrawal in August 1934. *Photomatic.*

which any intention so to treat the entire class was evidently rescinded. This led to the renumbering of the last three participants (BP Works Nos. 476/ 8/ 590) as shown in the following table:

Beyer Peacock Works No.	Original GWR No.	Built	Rebuilt as 0-6-0ST	First Post-Rebuild No.	Second Post-Rebuild No.	Converted to 0-6-0PT	Withdrawn
463	322	Oct-64	Jul-80	322	322	Apr-25	Oct-30
465	324	Oct-64	Dec-78	324	324 §	-	Apr-21
467	326	Oct-64	Sep-85	326	326	Nov-19	Oct-28
476	336	Nov-64	Jan-79	336	327 §	Oct-20	Mar-30
478	337	Nov-64	Feb-80	337	325	Aug-18	Mar-30
590	359	Apr-66	Dec-79	359	323 §	Feb-25	Jul-32

§ Initially fitted with condensing equipment for an indeterminate period.

The curvature in the running plate over the driving axles was an attractive, if outmoded, feature that distinguished this small class from the rest of the 0-6-0ST/ PT family. On becoming tank engines, all carried the Wolverhampton W3 boiler. Between February 1899 and December 1914, Nos. 323/ 5-7 received Wolverhampton R2 boilers (two rings, dome on front ring, raised firebox) while No. 324 was fitted with an R3 type [three rings, centre dome, raised firebox] in February 1898 which it retained until withdrawal. No. 322 acquired a Type S4 (two rings, back dome, flush firebox) in March 1914; Belpaire boiler was fitted concurrently with pannier tanks in April 1925. Nos. 322/ 3/ 5/ 7 carried superheated B4 boilers late in their careers, probably second-hand from 0-6-0 Armstrong or Dean Goods.

Despite their competence, the Beyers as tender engines acquired a mixture of cylinder dimensions and these were translated to the tank conversions: 17.5" x 26" (Nos. 322/3); 17" x 26" (Nos. 324/5/7); 17" x 24" (No. 326). There were cases of 0-6-0s sharing design and dimensional characteristics with more or less contemporaneous 0-6-0STs, as with the Swindon-built Armstrong Goods and the 'Buffalos'. However, tender/ tank conversions were unusual although it had occurred

with Class 59 0-6-0s Nos 60 & 67 (part of Swindon 1st Goods Lot) which were converted to 0-6-0STs at Wolverhampton in 1876/7 but reverted to tender engines in December and October 1886 respectively. During the period that conversions of classes 119 and 322 were effected, the 0-6-0ST type was in the ascendant with 'mass production' under way at both Swindon and Wolverhampton as evident in the table below.

Class:		119	322	1501	1076	1813
Works:		WV'N Rebuilt	WV'N Rebuilt	WV'N Built	SW'N Built	SW'N Built
Year:	1878	1	1	12	22	-
	1879	3	2	-	38	-
	1880	2	2	12	40	-
	1881	2	-	12	14	-
	1882	2	-	-	-	-
	1883	1	-	-	-	15
	1884	-	-	-	-	24
	1885	-	1	-	-	1
Total:		11	6	36	114	40

Above: Another undated view of No. 325 at Stafford Road. The outside frames and curved footplate made this variant arguably the most distinctive of the pre-Grouping saddle/ pannier tank classes. A further change saw it acquire a superheated B4 boiler in February 1925 in which condition it worked until February 1930.
W H Whitworth.

Against the intensity of this new build programme, conversion of 17 apparently capable 0-6-0s seemed a wasteful use of workshop resources. Application of the W3 boiler suggests that the exercise was an initiative by the northern works. With so many outstanding obligations in connection with the gauge question in the south, this episode raises questions about the wisdom of allowing George Armstrong so much latitude and also doubts about the efficiency of the company's divisional management structure.

Dimensional Comparison: Classes 119 and 322

Class	119	119	322	322
Frame Type	Sandwich outside/plate inside	Sandwich outside/plate inside	Double plate	Double plate
Boiler Type	S4	B4	R2 or R3	B4
Cylinders	17" x 24"	17" x 24"	17" x 26"	17½" x 26"
Heating Surfaces [sq ft]				
- tubes	1265	1059	1179	961
- firebox	101	99	102	106
Grate [sq ft]	17.3	17.3	15.5	15.5
Boiler Pressure [lb/sq in]	150	165	140	165
Driving Wheels	4' 7½"	4' 7½"	5' 0"	5' 2"
Tractive Effort [lb]	15,935	17,530	14,420	18,010
Wheelbase	7' 4" + 8' 4"	7' 4" + 8' 4"	8' 0" + 8' 3"	8' 0" + 8' 3"
Tank Capacity [gal]	circa 1080	1000	1100	1300
Weight [tons] §				
- leading	15.6 [11.5]	15.95	16.1 [11.45]	-
- driving	15.6 [10.3]	15.9	16.1 [11.45]	-
- trailing	15.6 [8.0]	13.25	12.9 [8.9]	-
- total	46.8 [29.9]	45.2	45.1 [31.8]	Not recorded

§ Comparative weights in brackets are for locomotives only in earlier tender form.

The 'Small' 0-6-0Ts

A parallel strain of new-build 0-6-0 tank engines was introduced at Wolverhampton in 1874, distinguished by the use of 4' 0" wheels which progressively increased to 4' 1½" diameter. This became another standard dimension albeit less widely used than that commonly associated with the large saddle/ pannier locomotives. These engines remained a Wolverhampton speciality with a total of 310 produced over the following 31 years. They were a useful, long-lived breed whose numbers relieved the GWR of the need to build more in that category during its independent existence.

Class 850

This class eventually totalled 170 locomotives and construction followed the normal pattern of Wolverhampton Lots comprising twelve each, plus the two renewals:

Loco Nos.	Works Nos.	Lot	Built
850-61	241-52	T	1874
862-73	253-64	V	1874/ 5
987-98	265-76	X	1875/ 6
93 / 94	Renewals	-	1875/ 7
1216-27	289-300	Y	1876/ 7
1901-12	410-21	J2	1881/ 2
1913-24	422-33	L2	1882
1925-36	446-57	O2	1883/ 4
1937-48	470-81	Q2	1886/ 7
1949-60	482-93	R2	1888
1961-72	500-11	T2	1889/ 90
1973-84	512-23	V2	1890/ 1
1985-96	527-38	X2	1891
1997-2008	539-50	Y2	1891/ 2
2009-20	551-62	Z2	1894/ 5

Introduction into service by year:

1874	17	1882	16	1888	12	1894	6
1875	18	1883	1	1889	6	1895	6
1876	8	1884	11	1890	15		
1877	7	1886	6	1891	20		
1881	8	1887	6	1892	7		

They resembled the large 0-6-0ST classes in the variety of boiler, cab and bunker styles and again reference to the RCTS work *Locomotives of the GWR: Part 5* is essential for definitive information on individual locomotives. For simplification, the class is reviewed here in three sections:

[1] the 48 locomotives of Lots T, V, X, Y Nos. 850-73/ 987-98/ 1216-27 [collectively No. 850 series].
[2] the two locomotives Nos 93/ 4 [the renewals].
[3] the 120 locomotives from Lot J2 onward Nos. 1901-2020 [collectively No. 1901 series].

On 27 November 1938, Class 850 No. 1220 was at Swindon in probably the most modern form that any class member achieved. Built in January 1877 with an R3 boiler, it graduated to an R4 version in November 1899 and was fitted with pannier tanks in July 1926 although a B4 boiler was first installed in August 1930. Enlarged bunkers with 2.5 tons capacity as in this case were introduced to the class from 1924 onwards. The enclosed cab and modern form of smokebox door is further evidence of up-grading although the early pattern buffers and original wheels have been retained. This locomotive was withdrawn in the month that this photograph was taken. *R C Riley (RCR 105).*

No. 850 Series

The Nos. 850-73/ 987-98 were built with R6 boilers (three rings and raised firebox). The dome was placed on the firebox with lock-up safety valves mounted on the dome cover. This unusual arrangement led to the mistaken assumption that they were domeless; replacement boilers of more conventional form were installed well before introduction of pannier tanks, and two versions used in replacement were:

• Type R3 (three rings, centre dome, raised firebox): Nos. 851/ 8/ 62/ 5/ 7/ 9/ 987/ 95/ 6. The first of this type was installed in No. 865 in November 1889. Nos. 1216-37 carried this boiler type from new.

• Type R4 (two rings, back dome, raised firebox): the remainder of the locomotives numbered between 850 and 998. All of Nos. 1216-27 batch had their R3 boilers replaced with this type after around 20-25 years. Significantly, this was a Swindon design specifically intended for this class and the first was installed in No. 850 in September 1894.

In view of their long working lives, there seems to have been surprisingly few later changes in boiler type which suggests that individual recorded histories may be incomplete. Thirty-five (Nos. 850-4/ 6/ 8-61/ 3/ 6-72/ 987-9/ 92/ 3/ 5-8/ 1217-21/ 4/ 5/ 7) later acquired B4 boilers, mainly in conjunction with fitting of pannier tanks. There were exceptions as with Nos. 855/ 64/ 73 which were sold while carrying R4 boilers and saddle tanks. Nos. 854/ 996-8 were fitted with pannier tanks a matter of years before Belpaire boilers were installed. Nos. 857 (Mar-21) and 862 [Dec-24] received pannier tanks in the months quoted but never acquired Belpaire boilers. Only Nos. 855/ 864/ 873/ 990/ 991/ 1216 remained as saddle tanks through their careers.

When built as saddle tanks, the footplates were completely open, save for provision of spectacle plates but cabs were fitted from around 1880. By the end of their careers, many had received enclosed cabs while the remainder acquired the half-cab version. Wheels of that period had cast iron centres but with No. 1216 onward, the spokes were of H-section profile, apparently copied at Wolverhampton from locomotives of the neighbouring LNWR. Detail changes in features such as style of smokebox doors, chimney dimensions, position of tool boxes stood witness to how the external appearance evolved.

Renewals Nos. 93/ 4

Built at Swindon in 1860, these were the first 0-6-0Ts constructed by the GWR, and were immediately despatched to the company's northern reaches where they spent their entire careers. In addition to side tanks, they were reported as being fitted with well tanks which, judging by the drawing, must have been inserted between the frame, below the bunker. There was a largely discounted view that they may have worked for a period solely with a well tank. The drawing by Ahrons is considered essentially accurate.

They were totally renewed as saddle tanks at Wolverhampton in November 1875 and February 1877 respectively. Details of No. 93 suggest that it was then akin to the 850 series with an R6 boiler while No. 94 more resembled the 1901 variation with R3 boiler. No. 93 acquired a B4 boiler plus pannier tanks in May-July 1921; No. 94 graduated to an R4 in October 1899 and pannier tanks in March 1927. They worked until February 1931 and July 1932 respectively; the company seems to have tried virtually every possible tank option with the pair over their long lives.

No. 1901 Series

All 120 locomotives (numbered 1901-2020) were built with R3 boilers and most graduated next to Type R4, except for Nos. 1917/ 20/ 4/ 30/ 8/ 42/ 7/ 9/ 51/ 9/60/ 5/ 72/ 5/ 9/ 88/ 9/ 2001/ 6/ 8/ 12/ 3/ 9 which moved straight to B4. Most of the R4 boilers fitted to this and the earlier 850 series were newly built which is why so many received pannier tanks well in advance of Belpaire boilers i.e. the original saddle tanks were around 20-25 years older than the R4 boilers. Most maintenance continued to be carried out at Wolverhampton but a small number were processed at Swindon. Up to 1894, where new boilers were needed, these were built at the northern works and shipped south. Nos. 2012/ 3 were the first of Class 850 to be fitted with pannier tanks

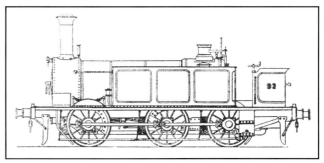

Nos. 93 and 94, the first 0-6-0Ts associated with the Northern Division, were actually built by Gooch at Swindon under Lot 'Two NG Tanks' in October 1860, before there were adequate facilities at Wolverhampton to undertake such work. Following delivery on transporter wagons, they apparently always worked in the north. They were renewed as saddle tanks at Stafford Road in November 1875 and February 1877 respectively and absorbed into Class 850 while retaining their original numbers. 'Renewal' in this case appears to have been a loose term as the wheel spacings were changed from 7' 6" + 6' 0" to 7' 4" + 6' 4" which meant frame replacement so probably little of the originals remained at this stage. They were in service as part of Class 850 until 1931/ 2 respectively.   *Drawing by Ahrons.*

in August and November 1910 respectively, concurrent with installation of B4 Belpaire boilers.

Subject to the caveat that individual histories may be incomplete, the broad pattern of later changes followed that set by the 850 series and only Nos. 1904/ 13/ 25/ 32/ 3/ 9/ 44/ 63/ 81/ 4/ 2007 retained R4 boilers and saddle tanks until withdrawal. There were instances of pannier tanks being installed years in advance of B4 boilers (Nos. 1220/ 1902/ 5/ 12/ 55/ 7/ 62/ 4/ 7/ 80/ 2010/ 5/ 7) and of pannier tanks fitted to engines that never acquired Belpaire boilers (Nos. 1222/ 3/ 6/ 1901/ 14/ 29/ 40/ 52/ 61/ 71/ 7). The 1901 series was distinguished by having the luxury of half-cabs from new and many graduated to the fully enclosed version later in their careers.

Above: No. 2012 ran with an R3 Type boiler and saddle tank from construction in November 1894 until receiving a B4 Belpaire boiler and pannier tanks in July 1910. This official photograph, which was probably taken following that works visit, depicts the superb standard of finish applied before World War 1 even to humble tank locomotives. In addition to the insignia on the tank sides, lining has been applied. The wide diameter of the tank equalisation pipe is evident in contrast to the less obtrusive and narrower diameter normal with a saddle tank. With the latter, the single centrally placed filler would allow equal distribution of water thereby naturally making replenishment faster. This locomotive had the distinction of being the last of Class 850 in service having been transferred from Llanelly to Birkenhead in April 1955 from where it was withdrawn in June 1958.

The class generally saw progressive increases in cylinder diameters from the original 15" to 16.25"/ 16.5" plus some cases of 17". Visually there was evidence of attempts to relieve cramped conditions at the rear end by frame extensions of 6" or 9". There appears to be no clear record of how many locomotives were so modified or when, and it is difficult to identify individual cases in the three-quarter angle photographs. These modifications suggest a tendency to employ engines on longer distance duties than the shunting/ pilot/ local suburban work that would have been expected of the type.

These diminutive engines in original form weighed 30.8 tons. Their maximum axle loading of 10.9 tons together with 15' 8" wheelbase permitted wide route availability but later modifications suggest that the all-up weight rose to around 35 tons. From the outset, they found work throughout the standard gauge network, especially over lightly laid and sharply curved lines in docks and industrial areas. More details will be provided in a later instalment that will review allocation and deployment of the pannier tank fleet generally.

Including the shortened careers of some members of Class 850 following their sale to colliery and industrial operators, their average working life was 54 years while in GWR service. The shortest was No. 855 (1874-1932) while some exceeded 60 years and two worked for even longer – No. 992 (76 years) and No. 1903 (71 years). Eight were sold were sold mid-career between 1906 and 1939.

Above: Class 850 No. 2010 was at Whitland on 31 July 1951, but later became a member of the Birkenhead platoon from whence it was withdrawn in August 1956. This engine was fitted with pannier tanks in April 1915 although it retained its round-topped R4 boiler until November 1935. In this scene it has also acquired enclosed cab and Collett-type bunker. This view is useful in showing how diminutive were these engines compared with the bunker of Class 8750 No. 3701 to the left and in exhibiting its H-profile driving wheel spokes. This feature was unusual on the GWR and Wolverhampton works might have adopted this design, inspired by its use on the neighbouring London & North Western Railway. *R C Riley (RCR 3322).*

Class 2021

Construction of small 0-6-0STs was revived at Wolverhampton after a two-year interval with production schedules changed to batches of ten or twenty in preference to the earlier discipline of twelve locomotives per Lot:

Loco Nos.	Works Nos.	Lot	Built
2021-30	623-34	D3	1897
2031-40	635-44	F3	1897/8
2041-60	645-64	G3	1898/9
2061-80	665-84	H3	1899/1900
2081-2100	685-704	J3	1900/1
2101-20	705-24	K3	1902/3
2121-40	725-44	L3	1903/4
2141-60	745-64	M3	1904/5

Introduction into service by year:

1897	14	1900	11	1903	19
1898	20	1901	15	1904	18
1899	20	1902	19	1905	4

There was continued operator appetite for locomotives of this useful size and compared with Class 850, a more intense pace of delivery was possible as production of larger 0-6-0STs (Class 655) and 0-4-2Ts (Class 3571) had concluded at Wolverhampton in 1897.

Class 2021 marked a pivotal stage in the Pannier Story as Nos. 2021-100 were the last GWR tank locomotives to be built for general service with round-topped boilers. Nos. 2101-60 crucially differed as the first 0-6-0Ts to carry the Belpaire boilers from new. Further, they were the last class to be built in substantial numbers at Wolverhampton, and the final 0-6-0ST type to be built by the GWR. With delivery of No. 2160, mass production of 0-6-0Ts paused and was not resumed until entry into service of 0-6-0PT Class 57xx exactly a quarter of a century later. (Note that these comments exclude the special case of the 0-6-0ST Class 1361, which is reviewed in the evolution of 0-6-0PT Class 1366 discussed in the Collett-era instalment).

The cramped rear end of Class 850 was probably that type's main drawback so this design was enlarged by lengthening the wheelbase by one foot. Other developments yielded increases in weight, carrying capacity and power output as recorded in the comparative table below. On construction, Class 2021 effectively comprised two types defined by their different initial boiler types so they are reviewed separately i.e. Nos. 2021-2100 (the 'No. 2021 series') and Nos. 2101-60 (the 'No. 2101 series').

Above: Class 2021 0-6-0ST No. 2112 as built in August 1902 with a Belpaire domeless type BR0 boiler. This was a classic example of the awkward profile combination of angular firebox and regular inner curve of the saddle tank. This was solved between July and September when the original boiler was replaced by a B4 Type and the saddle tank by panniers during what appears to have been a 6-8 week workshop visit. By timing differences in other cases, it is apparent that panniers were only installed once a saddle tank had been in use 20-25 years and was therefore probably life-expired. This locomotive reverted to a BR0 boiler for the period March 1925 to October 1929, and then carried another B4 until withdrawal in September 1954.

Above: Built in March 1902, Class 2021 0-6-0PT No. 2104 was at Tyseley in 1930 still carrying a BR0 domeless boiler. Note that compared with the previous view, the chimney is plain black and the safety valve bonnet has been painted green. The original saddle tank had been replaced by panniers in July 1927 but the boiler type was not changed until November 1937. The B4 Type then acquired remained until withdrawal in May 1951.

Below: Class 2021 No. 2027 was at Burry Port on 4 August 1951, retaining half cab and original bunker style. This locomotive later received a smokebox number plate and all black livery before withdrawal from Llanelly in February 1957.   *R C Riley (RCR 3372).*

No. 2021 Series

All eighty were built with Type R2/ 3 boilers (two rings of uneven length, dome on rear of leading ring, raised round-topped firebox). Ninety-six of these boilers, usually known as the 2021 type, were built between February 1897 and December 1906. Fifteen more were delivered November 1908 to December 1911. Excluding Class 1361, the last of this batch were the final round-topped boilers built by the company (delivery of Type R4 specifically intended for 0-4-2T Class 517 had been completed in March 1910).

The dates suggest that Type R2/ 3 boiler construction outpaced delivery of the 2021 series as some were also installed on Class 517 0-4-2Ts. This probably explains why adoption of Belpaire replacements commenced so early yet there were some cases of lengthy intervals before pannier tanks were fitted. Pre-Dec 1914 Belpaire installations and fitting of pannier tanks:

Loco No.	Date	Boiler Type	Pannier Tank Fitted
2021	Jan-06	BR0	Dec-36
2032	Apr-14	BR0	Sep-22
2037	Apr-14	BR0	Nov-22
2043	Sep-10	BR0	Dec-17
2050	Nov-14	BR0	Jun-25
2074	Mar-13	B4	Mar-13
2077	Oct-13	BR0	Oct-27
2084	Jan-06	BR0	Apr-18
2086	Dec-05	BR0	Jan-19
2087	Sep-12	B4	Nov-19
2097	May-14	BR0	Nov-22

Almost all the replacements were Belpaire boilers although the tradition of some curious change sequences was maintained. Summary of post-R2/3 changes:

B4 until withdrawal	2024/6/9/34/6/41/4-7/9/52-6/8/60/2/3/7-9/72-4/6/8-81/7/8/90/2-4/9	38
BR0 later B4	2021-3/7/31-3/5/7/40/2/3/8/50/1/9/61/4-6/70/5/7/82/4/9/91/6-8	30
BR0 until withdrawal	2028	1
BR2/3 later B4	2030/71/95	3
BR2/3 later R2/3 then B4	2038	1
BR0 later B4 then BR2/3	2025	1
B4 later BR0 then B4	2039	1
BR0 later R2/3	2083/2085/6	3
B4 later BR2/3	2100	1
Always R2/3 (sold 1907)	2057	1
Total		80

Two locomotives acquired BR0 boilers after only four years while the R2/3 type was much longer-lived in other cases e.g. No. 2034 (31 years), 2058 (30), 2063 (34), 2073 (33), 2094 (37). In contrast to the diversity of boilers used on earlier Wolverhampton classes, this series presented a simpler history. Excluding No. 2057 and noting that the R2/ 3 type would have been rotated within the series, all received Belpaire boilers at their first recorded type change. Between December 1905 (No. 2098) and March 1935 (No. 2023), thirty-one (Nos. 2021-3/7/31-3/5/7/40/2/3/8/50/1/9/61/4-6/70/75/77/82/4/5/9/91/6-8) gave up their R2/3 boilers for BR0 before finally acquiring Type B4. Between September 1912 (No.2087) and February 1938 (No.2094), thirty-eight (Nos.2024/6/9/34/6/41/4-7/9/52-6/8/60/2/3/7-9/72-4/ 6/78-81/7/8/90/2-4/9) acquired B4 boilers at their first change of boiler type, and retained them through to withdrawal.

Concerning adoption of pannier tanks, for the majority the practice largely continued of installing these together with B4 boilers during the same workshops visit, which could take up to two or three months judging by recorded dates. However, first conversion to Belpaire boilers did not always coincide with installation of pannier tanks:

Loco No.	BR0	B4	Pannier Tank Fitted
2023	Mar-35	Oct-33	Apr-25
2025	Apr-18	Feb-25	May-23
2027	Sep-19	Mar-23	Aug-23
2032	Apr-14	Dec-24	Sep-22
2035	Apr-15	May-36	May-36
2037	Apr-14	Oct-22	Nov-22
2038	[1]	Jan-36	Jan-27
2040	Jul-18	Nov-27	Jun-23
2042	Apr-18	Nov-38	Aug-23
2043	Sep-10	Sep-17	Dec-17
2048	Jul-18	Feb-48	Feb-48
2050	Nov-14	Jun-28	Jun-25
2051	Mar-23	Dec-28	Jun-23
2058	-	Oct-29	Feb-26
2059	Jul-16	Oct-31	Oct-24
2064	Mar-18	Apr-32	Aug-23
2075	Apr-18	Aug-34	Aug-34
2077	Oct-13	Oct-27	Oct-27
2082	Nov-19	Oct-27	Jan-26
2083	Nov-15	[2]	Jun-25
2084	Jan-06	Feb-18	Apr-18
2085	Jul-23	Mar-26	Sep-23
2086	Dec-05	[3]	Jan-19
2091	Jan-20	May-27	Dec-22
2094	-	Feb-38	Nov-29
2096	Oct-28	Jan-34	May-17
2097	May-14	Nov-22	Nov-22

Notes: **[1]** BR 2/3 boiler fitted Dec-26; R2/3 (Sep-29); B4 (Jan-36); pannier tanks fitted Jan-27.
[2] BR0 boiler fitted Nov-15; R2/3 (Jun-25); B4 (Jul-30); pannier tanks fitted Aug-25.
[3] BR0 boiler fitted Dec-05; R2/3 (Dec-10); B4 (Nov-18); pannier tanks fitted Jan-19.

The disparity in installation dates suggests an ad hoc approach to tank conversion. For example No. 2023 became a pannier tank eight years before it received a Belpaire boiler whereas No. 2048 was in service for 30 years with the Belpaire boiler/ saddle tank combination before receiving the more practical pannier tanks.

No. 2101 Series

The sixty locomotives of this series were all built with BR0 boilers, usually referred as the 'Class 2101' type (two rings, domeless, raised Belpaire firebox casing). The safety valve bonnet was mounted centrally on the boiler where the dome would normally be located. These boilers were built concurrent with their recipient chassis and discounting No. 2128 sold in 1911, their average working life was a little over 18 years. Graduation to the final B4 type commenced with No. 2130 in November 1912 and all the remainder were eventually so treated.

Regarding new construction of Belpaire-boilered locomotives, the chronology suggests poor communication between the two works considering:

- July 1903: 0-6-0ST (Swindon-built) No. 1813 acquired short version pannier tanks.
- March 1904: 0-6-0ST (Swindon-built) No. 2796 fitted with pannier tanks.

The final Lot (No. M3 of 1904/ 5) covering Nos. 2141-60 might have been more profitably built new with pannier tanks as by then the new concept had been proven, thereby eliminating the awkward marriage of saddle tank and Belpaire boiler. By this time JA Robinson was in command at Stafford Road but it seems that the independent culture fostered by George Armstrong still obtained.

This class was mainly built with new boilers and saddle tanks so broadly speaking, the transfer from R2/ 3 boilers (Nos. 2021-2100) to Belpaire boilers took place around 20-25 years from construction date.

Below: This view of No. 2034 at Worcester on 21 July 1954 is included to show how cab and bunker etc appeared from the rear, and to provide evidence of over-enthusiastic coaling! B4 boiler and panniers were fitted in November 1928 with withdrawal from Hereford in August 1955 after a career exceeding 57 years.
R C Riley (RCR 3262).

Left: Class 2021 No. 2151 stands at Machynlleth depot on 5 November 1946. This locomotive carried a B4 boiler and pannier tanks from July 1920 and was withdrawn in May 1952 from Danygraig. All but twenty of this class passed into British Railways hands but most were culled in the early 1950s. The final survivors were concentrated at Birkenhead for dock shunting duties and No. 2069 was the last half-cab pannier in service, withdrawn April 1959.
R C Riley (RCR 1254).

Post-Grouping Changes

The class was a favourite for auto-train workings from about 1905. Between February and April 1930, No. 2080 (equipped with pannier tanks and B4 boiler from June 1926) was experimentally fitted with 5' 2" wheels to assess suitability for this type of work at higher speeds. No. 2062 (pannier tanks and B4 boiler equipped January/February 1918) acquired auto-gear from No. 2160 in July 1930 and was withdrawn the following month for its frames and other components to be used in construction of the prototype for 0-6-0PT Class 54xx about which more information follows in a later instalment.

Already useful for a variety of localised and secondary duties it was felt that Class 2021's sphere of operations could be expanded by provision of greater brake power. Ten locomotives were so treated in 1939/ 40 and renumbered as sub-Class 2181:

New No.	Original No.	Converted	Withdrawn
2181	2133	Feb-39	Feb-52
2182	2125	Jul-39	Aug-55
2183	2074	Mar-39	May-55
2184	2145	Jun-39	Oct-50
2185	2149	Jul-39	Dec-52
2186	2118	Jul-39	Apr-55
2187	2143	Feb-39	Feb-52
2188	2087	Oct-39	Feb-52
2189	2189	Dec-39	Oct-50
2190	2190	Jan-40	Apr-51

Other Details

This popular class achieved average working careers of 50 years with the longest being Nos. 2027 and 2069 (both worked for 60 years) and the shortest were those of Nos. 2057 and 2128, both of which lasted only eight years with the GWR before sale.

Installation of pannier tanks commenced in November/ December 1912 with Nos. 2087/ 2125/ 30 concurrent with fitting of B4 boilers. Excluding the two early sales, the pannier tank installation programme was almost concluded in 1936 (No. 2021 in December; No. 2035 in May; No. 2107 in March) all of which concurrently received B4 boilers. By that year all but two had Belpaire boilers and pannier tanks. A late arrival was No. 2048 which carried a BR0 boiler and saddle tank from July 1918 until February 1948 when it was brought into line with a B4 and pannier tanks. Finally, honouring the tradition of there being a solitary exception No. 2028's history was built June 1897 with R2/3 boiler, acquired BR0 in February 1925 and was withdrawn still as a saddle tank in September 1938.

Their duties ranged from heroic haulage of heavy empty stock rakes at Paddington to penetration of obscure industrial sidings. With the latter, the load factor increased over time with heavier traffic patterns and greater wagon tares and load capacities. This flexibility underwrote their impressive longevity and was largely due to maximum adhesion. Class 517 0-4-2T was another long-lived Wolverhampton icon of similar diversity and the comparison table **(below)** demonstrates the importance of the adhesive factor.

Type	850	2021-2100	2101-60	No. 517 (As Introduced)	Class 517 (Final Version)
Weight per Axle [tons]					
- leading	10.9	13.55	14.3	9.9	10.6
- driving	10.9	13.6	14.25	9.35	11.8
- trailing	9	13.5	12.9	7.85	8.9
Adhesive Weight [tons]	30.8	40.65	41.45	19.25	22.4

With completion of Class 2021 No. 2160 in March 1905, the company's 0-6-0 tank engines for general service totalled almost 1,100. Generally speaking, life expectancy of around 40 years was considered acceptable for larger locomotives while longer, albeit indeterminate, careers were expected of smaller machines. Measured by average lives, the small saddle/ pannier tanks proved a hardy breed and a sound investment.

The principal specifications of the three main types as constructed:

Class/Series	850	2021-100	2101-60
Introduced	1874	1897	1902
Boiler Type	R3 or R4	R2/ 3	BR0
Cylinders	15" x 24"	16½" x 24"	16½" x 24"
Heating Surfaces [sq ft]			
- tubes	838	928	958
- firebox	78	93	96
Grate [sq ft]	13.3	14.5	14.7
Boiler Pressure [lb/ sq in]	140	150	165
Wheel Diameter	4' 0"	4' 1½"	4' 1½"
Wheelbase	7' 4" + 6' 4"	7' 4" + 7' 4"	7' 4" + 7' 4"
Weights per Axle [tons]			
- leading	10.9	13.55	14.3
- driving	10.9	13.6	14.25
- trailing	9	13.5	12.9
Total	30.8	40.65	41.45
Tractive Effort [85%] lb	13,350	16,830	18,515
Water Capacity [gallons]	644	900	900

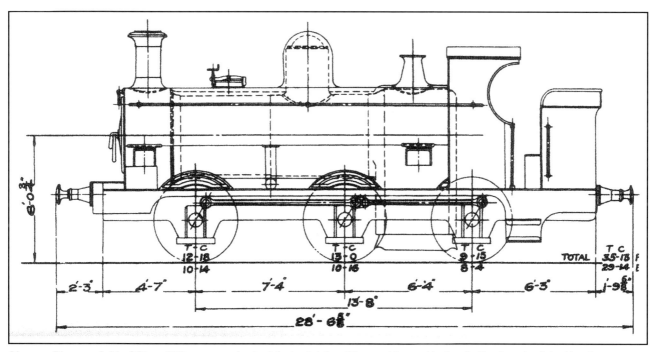

Above: Diagram A.31 of Class 850 as a pannier tank but retaining R4 round-topped boiler, half-cab and original bunker.

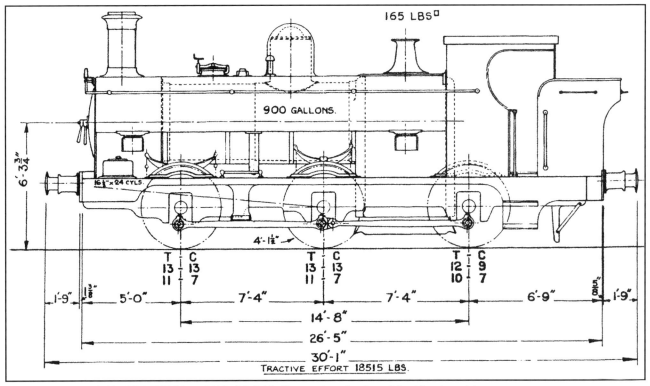

Above: Diagram A.38 of 0-6-0PT Class 2021 with B4 boiler, enclosed cab and final bunker style.

The final two images on this page show the full morphosis of the Wolverhampton Works rebuilding programme of the smaller 0-6-0 Saddle Tanks into Pannier Tanks. Extending the service life of somewhat antiquated looking 19th century designs, into the more recognised form of the modern Great Western shunting locomotive.

Left: Plenty of period detail in this view of 0-6-0ST Class 850 No. 2020 at Plymouth in 1921. The last of its class to be built, it emerged from Wolverhampton in May 1895. This locomotive originally carried an R3 Type boiler but provided the recorded dates are correct, here it is fitted with an R4 Type (two rings, back dome, raised firebox casing). Pannier tanks and a B4 boiler were fitted in October 1923. It was sold to Amalgamated Anthracite Collieries Ltd, Ammansford and by 1950 was at NCB Trimsaran Colliery.

Right: No. 1967 was long-in-the-tooth for an official portrait which displayed the GWR's final livery style. This engine is bereft of external toolboxes which have presumably been secreted in the cab. Obviously ex-works and destined for Llanelly depot, its last home from which it was withdrawn in June 1951.

The fourth instalment of 'The Pannier Story' will examine the Swindon pre-Grouping classes.

BOOK REVIEW

GREAT WESTERN RAILWAY DEAN 40FT VANS

ORIGINALLY COLLATED BY
BARRY SCOTT

Great Western Study Group (ISBN 978 191611 2216)
Softback, 72 Pages
£12.75

This is a compendium of articles written by J.N. Slinn and P.G.F. English published by the *Model Railway Constructor* in 1967, and based on research which the authors undertook for the Historical Model Railway Society. Also included is information provided in a later *MRC* article (November 1967) by Roy Miller which concentrated on the story of vans that formed Diagrams K.3 and K.4. With the concurrence of Ian Allan, this material has been combined, revised and extensively amplified by members of the Great Western Study Group who have added yet more information that was unavailable over half a century ago.

These vehicles are familiar through countless photographs which show them immediately behind the tender on mainline passenger trains, or perhaps accompanying vans intended for perishable traffic such as Siphons, Bloaters, Fruits on parcels or branch services. Their ubiquity stemmed from the number of years they were in service. The genre first appeared as wide-bodied broad gauge vans in 1882, followed the next year by 8 ft-wide bodies on broad gauge underframes (convertibles) and the last entered service in 1906 by which time almost 300 examples were in service.

In concept and basic design, they are simple vehicles (note the present tense as examples survive). However, this volume covers Diagrams K1 to 5, 11, 14 to 16, 24, 25, 28, 30 to 33/ L.7/ M.2, 4/ Q.14, 16 to 18 which provides a measure of their diversity in both original construction and later modifications. The amount of information provided within this 72-page volume is stunning with case histories providing dimensional details and mid-career modifications for 290 vehicles. There are seven pages of detailed line drawings which include variations in panelling, doors, windows, lookouts etc. Profusely illustrated and supported by authoritative commentaries, various designations are included concerning ordinary service duties, plus special tasks and later departmental work, thus: Ambulance train ward car, Breakdown train tender, Lamp van, Mess room, Newspaper van, Office, Post Office storage van, Parcel van, Parcels train brake, Pilot van, S & T Departmental van, Stores van, Tunnel inspection van.

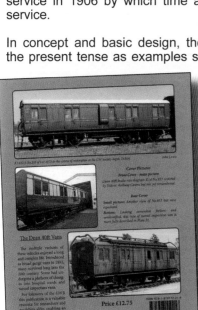

With the passing years, collation of the collective efforts of knowledgeable GWR historians sadly no longer around is a vital mission that provides invaluable sources of information for today's enthusiasts and for generations to come. Strongly recommended.

JPC

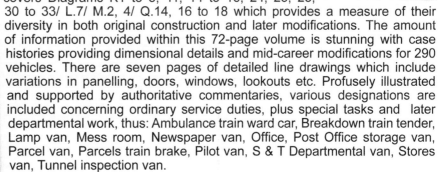

SNOW & ICE

There have been several winter episodes of note across the Great Western Railway network. The first, referred to as 'The Great Blizzard' of 1891 occurred over a five-day period in March but was sufficient to cause the death of 200 persons in Cornwall, 6,000 head of livestock and created drifts up to 15 feet high. Simultaneously at sea, gales left dozens of ships floundering on the Cornish rocks whilst inland a train was derailed near Camborne and another on the Princetown branch was buried completely. Despite a thaw setting in on 14 March the snow did not completely disappear from Dartmoor until June. Snow is also given as the associate cause for a number of other accidents that occurred on the GWR and BR(W) between 1840 and 1898 at Hammersmith Junction, 1867; Pontypool Road, 1873; Bishops Nympton & Molland, 1878; between Bristol and Salisbury, 1886; West Drayton, 1887; and finally at Tiverton Junction, 1898.

In the 20th century the years 1947 and 1963 will be recalled for extreme winters, the former not helped on the domestic front by prevailing austerity and a shortage of domestic coal for heating. This was also the year the bag from a water column purportedly froze whilst delivering water into the tender of an engine and despite the best efforts of many, the engine had to be declared a failure as any attempt to move it free was causing the actual column itself to shift in the ground. Harold Gasson also recalls wrapping cotton waste soaked in paraffin around the injector water feed pipes and that it was impossible to collect water from troughs as these were frozen solid.

In the same year 1947, the GWR experimented with two jet engines mounted on a wagon propelled over the line at Dowlais Top. The intention was that the heat and blast from the jets would clear snow. Unfortunately, the results were not exactly as had been expected for

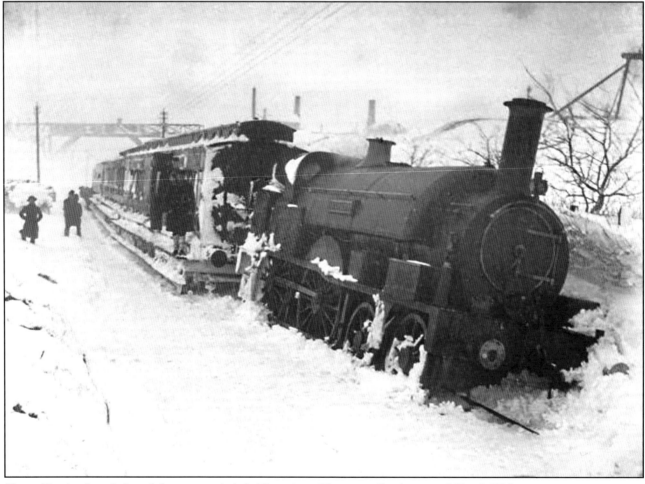

Above: The derailment of a relief passenger train in blizzard conditions near Camborne on 8 March 1891.

Snowed in on the Princetown branch between Burrator and Ingra Tor on 27 December 1927. Despite the best efforts of the hardy PW Gang, the preferred method of clearance under these circumstances was a plough fitted 0-6-0PT! *Great Western Society.*

whilst the jets may well have been successful in shifting fresh show, at Dowlais Top it was already well compacted, the heat and blast instead dislodging large chunks of snow and ballast to send these flying in various directions, folklore has it also setting light to creosote and oil soaked sleepers. A further difficulty and again referring to fresh snow, was the jets might well effectively clear what was in effect a tunnel through a drift but passage through this 'tunnel' was then fraught with danger for the operators who worked at the rear of the wagon upon which the jets were mounted. The subsequent official report produced by the National Gas Turbine Establishment commented that the test had to be abandoned at this stage owing to a severe risk the operatives might well suffer from asphyxiation.

'Snow Clearance with Jet Engines' was also the subject of an official government report produced in April 1947 by J McLean Tracy. The idea that a jet engine might be a useful means of snow clearance had been proposed by Dr Taylor, Chief Metallurgist at the National Gas Turbine Establishment at Whetstone. An initial demonstration unit mounted on a trailer gave promising results. Trials quickly established the jet was better at shifting show rather than melting it and six jet engine ploughs were assembled for either road and rail use. So far as road was concerned there were a number of obstacles to consider not least street

furniture and the potential for injury to pedestrians. The road jets were compared against bulldozers with the latter giving overall better results.

The first jet plough used on the GWR was built at Cardiff and fitted with two Rolls Royce Derwent engines. Tests commenced on Wednesday 27 February with the special working leaving Cardiff at 9.30am for Dowlais Top. Various tests were made on snow 6-12 inches deep with the jet engines running at 16,000 rpm. No results are mentioned. On the same day a report was received of a train derailed by ice 1-2 feet in depth with no location given. The jets were used to give the breakdown train a clear road and it was noted that it took four runs to afford effective clearance of the last 100 yards, the total running time for the jets (but not defined over a known distance) was 25 minutes. After this the unit returned to Cardiff.

From 26 February to Saturday 8 March, the unit was rerouted and worked from York, it returned to the GWR Newport (GWR) on Sunday 9 March. 'The following day a start was made clearing a line at Brynmawr. Some progress was made, about 200 yards being cleared in 35 minutes. Large lumps of snow were thrown about ten-feet into the air and one of these landed on the jet pipe which broke the chain suspension. As it was dark work was stopped for the day'.

On Tuesday 11 March an attempt was made to clear a line at Ebbw Vale where several points were blocked. There were failures of the machine on this occasion but eventually about a quarter of a mile was dealt with. The report then adds an interesting comment, '...as it was alongside the main road, the disruption to the life of Ebbw Vale grew to such proportions that is was deemed advisable to stop.'

The final entry was on 12 March when it was reported that with all blocked lines having been cleared by the GWR the view was expressed that the jet unit had not shown any improvement on the mechanical snow plough. In consequence it was again sent to York.

A second jet plough was built by the Southern Railway at Exmouth Junction in February 1947 and again fitted with a Derwent engine. There is no record if it ever did any snow-clearance work on the SR and instead was initially sent to York. It subsequently returned south and was also based with the GWR at Cardiff. On 9 and 10 March both units were operating independent of each other. Its time in South Wales was similar to the GWR version described above clearing the line in the area of Dowlais Central where a five mile section from Pontsticil to the I.C.I. Chemical Works was cleared in one and half hours. It was on the following day, 12 March that the conditions referred to in the main article were encountered; twelve-feet

drifts of wet and soggy snow, and during most of the running the complete plough was surrounded in a blanket of vapour and the instruments could not be seen at a distance of just 6 inches. When clearing wet snow there was no bursting as reported with dry snow hence the tunnel effect. This plough left the GWR on 13 March after which it is not believed any further clearance work using jet engines was attempted over GWR metals.

Move forward another 16 years into the BR era and some readers will recall the first few months of 1963. As in previous winters, the engine mounted snow ploughs were an essential component in dealing with the conditions. At this point we should explain that it is not believed the GWR ever possessed any specifically designed snow ploughs instead adopting the policy of having a locomotive(s) prepared for winter at various depots with a plough semi-permanently attached to the front. The engines used were invariably of the 0-6-0 type, tank or tender, the reason for this wheel arrangement being that driven wheels were less likely to become derailed in drifts and especially at points and crossing where compacted snow and ice might otherwise have built up between the check and running rails sufficient to lift a pony or bogie wheel and so cause a derailment. (The LMS at least, appeared to have a different perspective as to the type of engine that might be used with a plough).

A freezing cold Exeter St Davids on 12 January 1963. An unidentified '8750' Class 0-6-0PT has a snow plough attached and stands awaiting orders with the breakdown train Tool and Mess Vans behind. *Peter Gray*.

An unidentified 'Castle' makes dramatic progress through the wintery conditions on the Badminton line at Westerleigh. We have to admire the photographer for venturing out in such weather. *George Heiron*.

Points and crossings were a regular difficulty to keep clear, as witness a report in the February 1963 edition of the *Railway Observer* under the heading '1963 was not cold enough'. 'Western Region chemists do not consider that British winters are cold enough! During experiments on point de-icing fluid it has been established that frozen water binds the points to the rails as glue, and the freezing, thawing and re-freezing cycles, usual in this country, present difficulties not found in Canada the Alps and Scandinavia, where freezing is mostly continuous. A de-icing fluid has been produced which has the effect of releasing the ice, reducing corrosion and leaving a lubricating film which will keep points unaffected by frost for 18 hours. Tests are being carried out at Didcot, an area selected by the Meteorological Office.' (Didcot has long held the somewhat dubious distinction of being one of the coldest stations on the region; due to its proximity to the Berkshire Downs.)

If they were available, it would no doubt be fascinating to be able to read through the full set of GWR and WR control room logs covering various winter years to learn how the railway coped in such conditions. It is not even known if any of these survive and instead initial recourse has to be made, to various newspaper reports kindly located by Gerry Nichols.

From the *Torbay Express and South Devon Echo* of 3 January 1963; 'Three long distance trains due to leave Torquay today did not run. They were the 3.39am and the 10.40am to Cardiff and the 'Torbay Express', due to leave Torquay at 10.58am for London.

'At Newton Abbot railway station there were delays of up to half an hour in the restricted snow and fog rail service which came into operation on Monday.

'A railway spokesman said, 'We are clearing goods as quickly as possible and there is no undue delay to freight. During the past few days we have taken nearly 100 cars by rail to all parts of the country. Our great hazard is the clogging-up and the freezing of points. If we can keep them clear we should be able to maintain the restricted service.'

Five days later on 8 January, the same newspaper reported, 'The Kingsbridge-Brent railway line has been invaluable during the last 10 days, it is reported from Woodleigh, Gara Bridge, and Morleigh villages'. Mrs Rita Greig, the Woodleigh representative on Kingsbridge rural council, said the railway staff had been most helpful during the recent crisis and had willingly co-operated by delivering supplies of food along the route wherever they were required. It was estimated that over 1,000 people had used the branch line since the blizzard began. Notwithstanding this fall back on railway use, memories were destined to be short for both the residents and the WR as the Kingsbridge branch would close nine months later in September 1963.

Left: Saturday 29 December 1962 saw the last day of public services on the Launceston branch from Plymouth, a historical event accompanied by a thick blanket covering of snow. Laira's Small Prairie No. 5564 is seen at Tavistock South, adorned with a commemorative headboard. This was not quite the end of the story however, as the big freeze led to the abandonment of the timetable and it was into the New Year before all the trains were recovered back to Plymouth. *Bernard Mills.*

Opposite Right: Torre station is recorded in sub-zero conditions on 11 February 1963. An unidentified North British D63xx diesel-hydraulic gingerly approaches on the 8.15am Newton Abbot (Hackney Yard) to Goodrington freight working. The crew must surely have been appreciating one of the benefits of dieselisation within the heated cab. *Peter Gray.*

Below: Intrepid passengers at Tiverton alighting from the 11.23am ex Tiverton Junction on 2 February 1963. The steam heating provision is clearly being put to good use within the saloon of Hawksworth auto-trailer No. W224W. *Peter Gray.*

Elsewhere in Devon where the Southern main line skirted Dartmoor it was far worse with three engines stuck fast between Meldon and Bridestow west of Okehampton; despite the best efforts of ploughs it was human muscle power that was to prove the most effective solution – and lighting fires underneath to thaw out frozen wheels and motion.

North and east on the Cheddar Valley line three engines coupled together failed to clear a route through near Easton, north of Wells and they too eventually became trapped when cleared snow fell on to the previously cleared line behind them. (The nearby Somerset & Dorset line similarly fared badly around this time.) It is likely almost every other BR(W) line could recount its own tale.

Steam to Diesel and Back to Steam Again

In January 1963 water columns at Monmouth Troy froze and the pannier tank which had worked a freight service from Chepstow had to have its tanks replenished courtesy of the local fire brigade. After this a diesel shunter was used.

Elsewhere in the same period there was a heavy influx of steam at Laira necessary to replace a higher than usual number of weather related diesel failures. As this was also the time of the general change over from steam to diesel traction and consequently owing to staff redundancies, Laira could not cope and steam engines were instead sent to Friary for servicing.

The extreme weather conditions of the period also caused the curtailment of the daily freight from Merthyr to Brecon. On one occasion this was due to an estimated 50 tons of snow and ice overhanging the northern portal of Torpantau tunnel making it impassable to traffic. The line was cleared after staff from Merthyr worked all day on the blockage.

It fell to the various members of the permanent way gangs to try and keep the tracks clear although once a turnout was cleared sufficiently for the passage of a train, this same train could then blow the cleared snow back again. Copious supplies of salt were also sometimes stored in the corrugated huts more usually kept for lamp oil; the subsequent effect of the salt on the metal may be imagined. In conditions of falling snow, the same p/way men were kept busy acting as fogmen; this duty requiring a man to be stationed at the distant signal and place a detonator on the rail when the distant arm was 'on'. Should a train approach the fogman would also display a yellow aspect from his handlamp to the driver as an added warning. If the distant signal was 'off' the detonator was removed. Regulation 5 'Section Clear but Station/Junction Blocked' was suspended in snow conditions and in consequence where this was otherwise in force services were instead worked under Regulation 4 meaning further delayed. Signalman were expected to regularly operate points and locks that were in frequent use again in an attempt to keep these operational and snow free.

WESTERN TIMES

The *Western Region British Railways Magazine* for February and also March 1963, carried articles on the effect the winter weather was having on the region. In the February issue the topics were in the main general but with some specifics included. These included facts such as in the Midlands (the WR still having its own Midlands division at that time) 94 main line passenger services were able to operate on 29 December 1962 out of the usual total of 101. The majority of engines available were used on passenger services, with priority given to suburban workings.

At Old Oak Common the weather badly affected a number of points meaning there was difficulty in getting engines out of the depot. Propaganda too played its part – 'modern propaganda' – that is, as mention was made of frozen (steam) locomotive injector feeds, '....but diesels stood up to the test well since they could be kept active most of the time.'

A difficulty not always considered was that of rostering; footplate staff finishing their duty late had to have their next turn of duty suitably adjusted whilst again at Old Oak, with many cases staff lived outside the area and were thus dependent upon public transport to reach the depot – public transport that was often unreliable in such conditions.

Outside on the line track circuit failures become common due to low insulation between the running lines and over the top of Box Tunnel telegraph wires were broken when branches fouled the wires. (Perhaps we had not realised that the 'pole-route' went over the top of the tunnel.)

The March edition of the same magazine contained a more detailed survey of events. 'The year of 1963 has already made certain that it will not be forgotten – it has ushered in the bitterest weather spell of the century so far. The winter of 1947 was a landmark in Arctic conditions, but there was one saving grace on that occasion – there was a let-up during daylight hours. This time there has been none. The freeze-up has persisted all the time, and the depth of cold has been such that locos have frozen while running during the day. That is something this region has never experienced before. But we are proud to record that the men and women of the Western have won through this great ordeal, and it is gratifying to record the words of Mr James Griffiths, MP for Llanelly, in the House of Commons on 24 January: "In weather of the most severe kind, Wales has had to depend upon her railways, and all those connected with the railways deserve the public's sincerest congratulations for the way they were keeping the services going."

The Toughest Weather Story of the Century

'There was hardly time to breathe the usual sigh of relief on Boxing Day before the snow came down, 24 hours late for the children and all too soon for the grown-ups.

Above: Trains are seen crossing at Marsh Mills on 29 December 1962. Push-pull fitted autotank No.6430 is providing the power for the 2.10pm Plymouth-Tavistock service, which a flurry of passengers seem keen to board to escape the bitter cold.

'By the following morning drivers and guards, signalmen and gangers, porters and booking clerks were having difficulty in getting to their depots and stations. If a few trains were delayed (the Western Region was just finishing off the running of 109 extras over the holidays) there were few complaints. There was snow about, after all. Everybody could see that. And it had happened before.

What Else Was to Come?

'The night after that more snow fell. London and Bristol took the worst of it on this region. Five westbound and twelve eastbound expresses had to be cancelled, and the London division operated a restricted service. Next morning snow was still falling down in the west country, restricted services were still the order of the day at Paddington and, because the experts gave no hope of a break, railwaymen everywhere were on the verge of wondering what was coming now.

'They found out soon enough. More snow, up to the rail-tops and with the snow – fog, mainly in the Midlands. Then more snow and still more snow. A six-foot drift blocked the line at Ashendon Junction early on the Sunday morning and the ploughs were ordered out to clear it. They got through the huge soft banks of white late that evening and the line was open again by half past nine. (While they ploughed, the northern route trains were diverted via Oxford.)

'Meanwhile, overnight trains from several points of the Western Region compass were heavily delayed, and if the snow eased off elsewhere it turned to sleet in Swansea. Frozen points outside Paddington meant a late start to seven trains. A thousand things began to happen all at once.

Snow Ploughs Out All Night

'On the last day of the old year the 9.35pm freight from Banbury to Southall ran slap into a drift about a mile north of Haddenham, on the London-Birmingham route, and was only rescued at 5.30 in the morning by the Southall snow plough after a refrigerated stay of more than three hours. The 8.25pm Shrewsbury to Marylebone milk train was held up behind the freight, and that repercussed back along the line to make a number of cancellations.

'Down in the Vale of Glamorgan other snow ploughs were out all night, too, and between Yate and Westerleigh, as well as between Evercreech and Midsomer Norton, there seemed to be a wall of white looming up into the sky. But the railwaymen were there, while the millions slept in warm beds, with nothing promised except tears and toil.

'Then came the respite, like the end of a journey through a long cold tunnel, the lovely sound of snow melting into water, and the water running into the drains.

Trains await their turn away from Badminton, where undoubtably the best place to be was in the Restaurant Car! *George Heiron.*

Resident '8750' Class No. 4658 simmers away inside the Laira roundhouse on 29 December 1962. These 0-6-0PTs fitted with such rudimentary ploughs were vital in keeping the trains running. The photographer diligently noted, '…it was snowing outside…!'. *Peter Gray.*

Prepared for a potentially essential duty, a work-stained Collett 0-6-0 No. 2287 stands at Gloucester Horton Road shed on 15 February 1964. As with the plough fitted to the front of the pannier tank seen earlier, how was the smokebox cleaned with the attachment in place and how long was a plough engine kept in steam before it needed a boiler wash out?   *R H G Simpson.*

'Everyone hoped that this heralded the end of just another bad spell, not a bit of it. More snow blotted those hopes right out. Ashendon Junction got it again, and again expresses went through Oxford instead. The main line between Castle Cary and Taunton was impassable, the snow ploughs thrust their sharp noses into the cold once more, and delays mounted up into a heavy overdraft of time lost.

'And so the story went on. The snow fell, froze on the ground, laid off for a few hours, fell again and froze again on top of the first layer. As fast as the points were cleared – by hand, often ungloved, and on two feet, often lumps of ice – they were filled in again -and were cleared again.

'If a guard, a driver, a signalman or a shunter reached his depot somewhere near right time for duty one day, there was no guarantee he could make it the next, though it was never for lack of trying. (There is even a story of a porter who walked five miles down a line to see if any drifts would stop a train getting through. At six on a deathly cold morning, too.)

'If an engine, even a steam engine, wasn't frozen one night, no one could predict – even with fires in the pits underneath – that it would be as lucky on the following night.

'Keep the lines free, that was the first essential all the time, a wicked enough job in the first phase of soft snow, a near-impossible one in the later freeze-up stage which lasted for weeks and shook railwaymen of 40 and 45 years' service into admitting that they had never known conditions like these.

'But before you work on this keep-the-lines-free theory you have to know where the stoppages are, and this is where HQ Control comes in, that ordinary-looking railway office which has perhaps a dozen more telephones than usual. Control is the nerve centre of the region in snow, fog, black ice or blue skies. Smaller control points along the line report news of happenings locally – the freight wagon off the rails in Wales, the engine failure in Gloucestershire, the effects of other upsets in other regions which have still other effects on our own – anything and everything.

'It is Control's business to know about and study every cause of delay and minimise – or, at best, avoid altogether – the effects on following trains. Even in normal conditions they have to think fast and far ahead. In sub-normal conditions they have a field day, which in this case lasted without a break for weeks.

'In the afternoon of 22 January, the Birmingham Pullman, heading for London, was held up at Haddenham by an engine failure in the diesel hauling the 8.55 am Birkenhead train just in front of it. When Control got the news it was already too late to do anything about the Pullman, because it was hot on the tail of the 8.55 anyway. But Control could – and did, for

this is the essence of its function – think and act ahead to prevent the first cause of delay reacting on the third train, from Aberystwyth. So Birmingham was told the story and the Aberystwyth train was diverted; Southall produced a pilot to help the crippled 8.55, which was pulled out of the way temporarily; then the Pullman went past it, the 8.55 following on.

'This sort of action-on-information is normal when conditions are fair. It happens every half hour. But in snow and prolonged freeze-ups it is multiplied twenty times over. "Drifts at point A", comes the information. What's the action? Call the snow plough out. Three trains are heading for the drift – which of them can we divert? Too late to stop the first one, but can we do something about the other two? Then, "More drifts at points B and C" – but the plough for that area is already being used. What now? We'll have to wait. Everybody will have to wait until we can spare it. Something has to give. When things are bad, it's a question of working from moment to moment, of cutting the suit according to the cloth.

Above: The use of diesel traction may be noted on this 1963 BR(W) poster, but then this was the time when the failure of a diesel was referred to publicly as 'a locomotive failure', no specific mention of diesel difficulties being permitted.

The Brutal Situation

'Keep the lines free'. Four short words, like 'take a deep breath'. But what a host of things are involved behind it. Frozen points, for instance. The snow falls, a man with a shovel pushes it away. The snow still falls, the man still keeps shovelling. One point is bad enough, an endless task in itself as long as the snow keeps on. But twenty points? And only two men because the third (and the fourth and fifth) never got to the station? Can they win? Yes, given half the chance. But they don't get even that when all anyone need do is breathe on a window and watch it freeze.

'Streamline your services, nurse your motive and man power, cut according to the cloth. More high-sounding words. You have already cut your cloth according to the brutal situation, you have already cut the long-distance passenger services down to the bone, transferred men and locos to the freight side, given top priority to the lines for food and fuel. Yet what happens if those men are driving a steam engine at the head of a freight and even while they are running the injector, which takes the water from the tender to the boiler, freezes solid? (No injector – no water for the boiler. Hot fire under waterless boiler – boom! No engine.) Has it ever happened before? Yes, but not to the extent it happened in the third week in January 1963. It was all over the region. What do you do?

"Well," said a Welsh driver, "you do the best you can, like. You get a bit of cotton waste, see, and stick it in the old oil can and light it up and see if you can thaw the thing out. You haven't got asbestos hands, see, with which to pick up red-hot coals from the fire now, have you? So you do the best you can. If you don't win, you have to drop the fire. You're dead then, see. Dead as a duck. You sit there and wait for help – after you've chucked the fire outside with the shovel first. And there's crazy for you. Sitting there watching a nice big hot fire die in the cold, and you along with it. There's crazy."

'How do you plan trips for steam engines when all the water troughs on every route are frozen into strips of pack ice? You skip the troughs altogether, of course, and stop at the next station. What happens when the water column is frozen solid, too? You're dead. Dead as a duck. You do the best you can. Control has to find another engine from somewhere – if Control can, if that one isn't frozen solid too.

"I can't do without water any better than a housewife can," said a restaurant car chef. He pointed at the floor. "My tank's under there and the pump's frozen. If I don't see a 10 lb pressure on that gauge I don't see water either. What do I do? I get some milk churns, fill 'em before we start off and keep 'em filled every station we stop at. Last week I did about 130 breakfasts, nearly 60 lunches and something like 90 dinners that way."

"And see that metal lining above the toaster? It should be full of water, otherwise the roof burns away – the water's an insulator. But there's been none in it for three weeks now, and no toast for the passengers either. We put rolls in the oven and heat them up instead. No complaints. We do the best we can. You can't do more, can you?" In January 1963 hundreds of restaurant cars were affected in the same way.

'On Paddington's Platform 2 there is a group of men who look after the steam and vacuum pipes on all the trains. They, like every other railwayman at the blunt end of the work in that weather, had no let-up. One of them was holding a train heating pipe against a spout of a boiling kettle. The pipe was packed with ice.

"How many we've had like this?" He laughed. "None of us here could count up. Every minute of the day you can have everything come on you like a ton of bricks. It isn't these pipes so much, it's the valves on the coach side of them. They freeze up. You can get a train off Old Oak Common, where it's been heated first anyway, but by the time it's got here there's no heat anywhere. That valve on the last coach coming in is the valve of the first coach going out, so when that freezes, and even when you've got the engine on, the heat doesn't get past the tender.

"What do we do? Borrow a blowlamp and try and thaw it out. Trouble is, the steam pipes go under the coach floors and if they get frozen you can't use a blowlamp there unless you want to set the whole train alight. What do we do then? The best we can. If we don't win the trains have to go out cold." January 1963 was the worst they experienced.

Vital Test For the Shunter

'Marshalling yards did not escape the cold. With those bitter winds shrieking across the open ground, perhaps they got the worst of it. The ground at night looks harmless and even. In fact, it's lumpy and deadly. A string of wagons comes rolling past the shunter, and he runs alongside it, using the pole to uncouple them. Every wagon now, whether full or empty, is vital. And every running step the shunter makes is vital, too. Freezing hands, freezing ground, running feet. One slip . . . No shunter had fun in January 1963. A hammer was often the best tool – to crack the couplings loose. He did the best he could. There was nothing else for any railwayman to do.

'The factor which made all the difference this year was that we had more consecutive days of sub-zero temperatures (32 degrees of frost [Fahrenheit] in Shropshire during the night of the 23rd) than even in 1947. And, towards the end of January, it was this which began to threaten the freight lifeline, the very aspect of railway transport which had been given top priority earlier on.

Above: Railway operations across the Principality of Wales were severely hampered by heavy snowfalls and persistent ice over a number of winters. One such typical scene is captured here at Cardiff General during December 1965.   *Bernard Mills*.

Below: The former L&NWR 'Central Wales' line, that came under BR(W) control upon nationalisation, was also prone to inflictions caused by the weather during the winter months. The lonely platform at Llangunllo is seen looking south on 14 February 1970.

WESTERN TIMES

Coal Turns Into Concrete

'Moving coal at all became a tremendous problem. It froze solid, like everything else, in the wagons and on the ground. Jets of steam did no more than soften the top twelve inches. Firemen had to fight for every shovelful from the tenders. Traders found it impossible to off-load railway wagons, and even if they succeeded the roads were so bad that they never reached the back streets.

'So the vital contents of the wagons remained locked in the deep freeze, unusable. So the wagons were useless, too. The collieries kept turning out more coal and, with fewer and fewer wagons to load, were forced to stack on the ground – where it froze. To save what there was to be saved, our restricted services were restricted further still while carriages and engines continually froze as hard as the coal heaps. It was a vicious and critical circle.

'Yet for all the difficulties, trains did run, some of them even to time. Coal did move, somehow. Failures in motive power and on the track were overcome, somehow. Even long-distance trains did well – in the circumstances. If you had to go to Wales from Scotland or to London from Penzance, you could – in spite of the fact that everyone knew, in the third January week, that we never had it so bad.

'Was there no more than very cold comfort here? Yes. The public was appreciative. In the worst of the weather double the usual number of people wrote in to say so. One excerpt can speak for them all from the father of a teenage daughter who was travelling to Truro early in January: "When some people quibble about rail fares I say this journey and the relief was worth £20 to me and I thank everybody responsible." Who was responsible? The men on the line. They did all right. Better than that, they did marvels.'

More recently and certainly outside the time line for *Western Times*, the term 'the wrong type of snow' has become a widespread euphemism to describe the excuses used by the transport network when a particular weather phenomenon disrupts traffic. Whilst the term was first used in the early 1990s it was the same physical issues, i.e. light powdery snow, had befallen the diesels at Laira thirty years before.

Interesting to note also that post steam the BR(W) had finally got around to owning some independent snow ploughs, no doubt necessary to prevent the ingress of snow to bogies and traction motors of the propelling engine.

Other tribulations caused by 'Mother Nature' to railway operations, will be documented in future issues.

Above: We conclude this examination of snow and ice across the Great Western network, with this chilling photograph taken at one of its most iconic locations. On 11 December 1966, Derby built 'Peak' Class diesel-electric No. D35 is in the process of being removed from an inter-regional express at Bristol Temple Meads. The locomotive was allocated to Leeds Holbeck at this date.   *Bernard Mills*.

THE MISSING SIGNAL

In the Minutes of Proceedings of the Institution of Civil Engineers for 1910/11, Alfred Thomas Blackall M. Inst. C.E of the GWR submitted a paper *Modern Railway Signalling; Some Developments on the Great Western Railway*. (The name Blackall was synonymous with the GWR and the signal department, various branches of the family serving in the Signalling and Traffic Departments in the Reading area).

In his discourse Mr Blackall referred to progress in signalling as well as interlocking and perhaps most interesting to readers the reason for, the type of, and the positioning of signals. The paper runs to some 20 sides which apart from the technical, included reference to one type of signal which was a rare beast indeed. Fortunately, Mr Blackall provides a drawing and explanation whilst if any reader possesses an image of such a signal the editors would be most interested.

To quote, 'A goods-loop train-indicator is used for the purpose of warning the driver of the condition of a refuge-loop which he may be entering whether any, and, if so, how many trains are already in the loop. The Author has designed the indicator shown which is to be fixed upon the post of the signal for entering the loop. The case upon the signal-post contains a circular 'window' in which numbers appear, corresponding with the number of trains admitted into the loop. The disc carrying the numbers is revolved by means of a lever in the signal box. There are notches in the curved (quadrant) guide of the lever, corresponding with the number of trains which the loop will hold; and the numbers upon the disc correspond with these notches. When the loop is empty, the lever is in its normal position, and '0' appears in the window. A train having been sent into the loop, the signalman pulls the lever to the first notch, which causes the disc to revolve partially, when '1' appears in the window; and so on until the maximum number of trains the loop will hold is reached. A lamp inside the case illuminates the window at night.' Goods loops had by this time also begun to replace refuge sidings in several places not least due to the time taken to stop a train and for it to (slowly) set back clear of the running line could be considerable. David Smith (see below) comments that 'Such loops were known at this time as Avoiding Lines'.

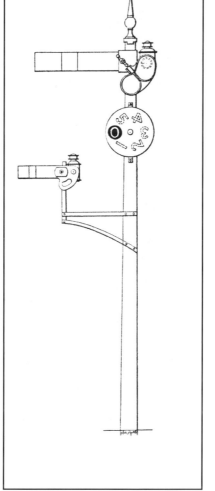

The paragraph above immediately raises a question. The lever containing the notches must have been separate from the lever controlling the signal allowing access to the loop; otherwise, there would have been no means of restoring the signal arm to 'on'; we are likely too early in history to consider a track circuit in advance of the signal as being used to return the arm. In addition to the position of the notched lever was there in addition an instrument on the block shelf repeating the position of the lever, and was this notched lever interlocked in any way with others?

The late David Smith in his scholarly tome *GWR Signalling Practice* (GW Study Group 2019 – highly recommended), refers to one such indicator being fitted to the up main inner home signal at Maindee Junction East in 1907. Smith includes a copy of the same drawing accompanying the present article but no actual photograph. We are not told how long it survived but perhaps confirming its unusual status it is specifically referred to on p.126 of the GWR Appendix to No. 7 Section of the Service Time Tables dated March 1941 (UFN) under the heading 'Mechanical Indicator for up loop line at Maindee Junction East signal box.' The text continues, 'A mechanical indicator showing how many trains (up to four) are in the up loop between Maindee Junction East and East Usk Junction signal boxes, is fixed to the up side of the up loop line twenty yards in advance of Maindee Junction East signal box.' It is not known how long it remained, possibly until the respective signal boxes were both closed on 16 April 1961. (No image has been found when scouring the various books covering the Newport area.)

Above: Drawing from Mr Blackall's lecture. The position of the disc on the main doll is interesting as presumably this particular signal refers to the main running line. Perhaps it was simply a case of there being no space, on this example at least, for the disc to be placed on the doll supporting the shorter arm. Note too the latter is not a ringed arm.

The fact Smith advises the indicator at Newport was in place in 1907 tends to imply that Blackall's paper may also have been a little out of date when it was presented to the institute. We do know that the circular indicator case was 2' 6" in diameter with an 8" aperture which would show 7" numerals.

Such a signal may of course have been a unique offering 'in the flesh' (or should that be 'in the metal') so to speak,

although worth mentioning is that the GWR 'Red Book' of *Regulations for Train Signalling* dated 1936 records three closely types pages as to 'Regulations for Signalling Trains and Engines by Permissive Block System over Goods Running Loop Lines and Other Permissive Lines'. Included are special bell codes to cover such eventualities as a train on a permissive goods line being withdrawn from the rear.

Guards of stationary goods trains standing on a permissive line were instructed to alter the offside lamp on their van nearest the main line to white. More telling was that mention is made of a 'Tell Tale' instrument in the signal box which must show how many trains are occupying the loop. Might this reference to an 'instrument' simply have been the position of the lever in the quadrant or is it in fact confirmation of the writer's belief that the controlling signal box would also have a separate instrument repeating the position of the lever in the quadrant? This instrument likely to be based on, or similar to that illustrated.

With the potential for two, or more, trains on the same section of line the regulations go into detail so that (in railway terms but not a quote from the instructions) 'a clear understanding' is reached by all parties and each know their own responsibilities. Considering there was the potential for more than one train in the same section, hence the word, 'permissive', extreme caution was indeed required, for example the rules governing speed for example stating this must not exceed 10mph or 4mph in fog and falling snow. Even so and considering freight trains were mainly run unfitted at that time, stopping quickly even from 4mph could still be fraught with difficulty.

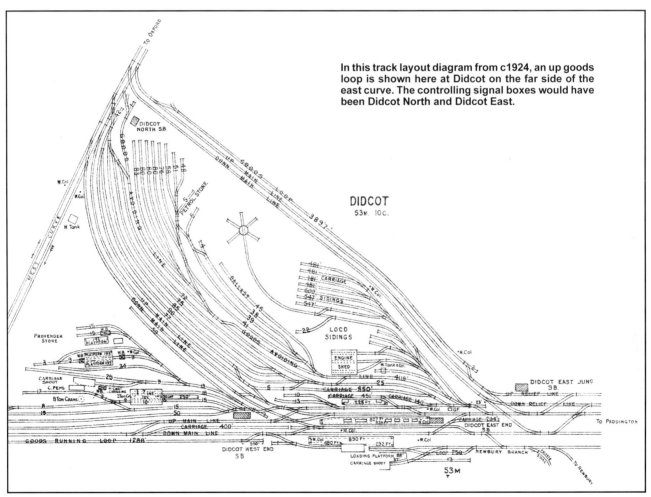

In this track layout diagram from c1924, an up goods loop is shown here at Didcot on the far side of the east curve. The controlling signal boxes would have been Didcot North and Didcot East.

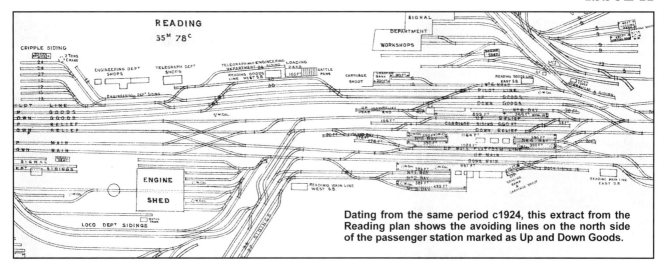

Dating from the same period c1924, this extract from the Reading plan shows the avoiding lines on the north side of the passenger station marked as Up and Down Goods.

Adrian Vaughan in his work *Great Western Signalling* (1973 reprinted 1984), refers to goods loop working thus, 'Under permissive regulations, a signalman at 'B' could accept a train from 'A' when the line was clear to the home signal; there was no clearing point. If the line was already occupied; the signalman at 'B' would acknowledge 'A's 'Is line clear?' with a single beat on the bell'. (There was of course a separate bell for a goods loop.) The (second or subsequent) train that was intended to enter the loop had to be stopped at the loop home signal so that the driver could be advised as to how many trains were ahead. This advice also included the exhibiting of a green flag/lamp to the driver – remember under these circumstances green meant 'caution'. Adrian adds, 'Sometimes an indicator was fitted to the signal post showing how many trains were in the loop', in which case the train need not be stopped as the appropriate message was automatically conveyed to the driver.

The next consideration is to where this regulation might apply and to this end we must consider where goods loops / goods running lines were located. Certainly, there were such lines at Reading, Bristol, Taunton, Exeter and elsewhere, whilst during WW2 certain former passenger lines were converted to goods loops 'for the duration'. This change also applied to companies other than the GWR at this time.

The signalling regulations were revised in the 'Green Book' issued by the BR(W) in 1960 and Permissive Block working was still mentioned. No accidents specifically related to permissive block working have been found recorded on the excellent Railways Archive website, but as reportable accidents invariably involved passenger lines and workings, any incidents that did occur may well have only been subject to an internal enquiry.

Before anyone writes in, we should also state that permissive working could apply on a passenger line as well; the example being when a train is at a platform, and it is necessary for another movement to take place at the rear i.e. attaching or detaching vehicles.

GWR pattern '1947' permissive block instrument. For the first train to enter the loop the commutator would be turned to the left, 'Line Clear', at which time the indicator needle would similarly more into the 'Green' segment. When the train was advised by the box in rear as being 'on line' the signalman would turn the commutator to 'Train on Line' which would simultaneously move the needle to the 'Red' segment. Subsequent trains would see the commutator turned to position 2,3,4,5, or 'Blocked Back' which meant the loop was full. As each train departed so the dial would be reversed by one. As trains were invariably of different lengths it does not mean six train could always be accommodated – indeed the number be far less. Different designs for instruments undertaking the same function existed, most being produced by Messrs Tyers although one permissive instrument is known of where a horizontal row of numbers was provided below the needle and without a commutator.

Many images of the Great Western cross the editorial desks of *Western Times*, but it is unusual for an image to cause the spontaneous and collective gasp of delight that was accorded this portrait of Dean Single No. 3003 *Avalanche* at Bristol circa 1900.

Built as a large and slightly ungainly 2-2-2 in February 1892, *Avalanche* was converted to a 4-2-2 in May 1894 and remained in this form until withdrawal February 1909. (The history of William Dean's masterpiece was outlined in *Western Times* Issues 3 & 4).

ENGLISH SIGNAL BOXES IN COLOUR

The humble signal box was often overlooked by photographers, especially when using expensive colour film. This selection taken from across the GWR's English network, is intended to provide some extra detail for infrastructure historians and modellers alike. A further offering from Wales will appear in the next issue.

Above: *Teignmouth Old Quay Signal Box*. A standard GWR Type 5 design opened in 1889 and seen here in 1968. *Bernard Mills*.

Above: *Mount Gould Junction* signal box on 10 November 1973. Opened in 1891 with 25-levers, it controlled the GWR's Plymouth No.1 curve access into Friary station and No.2 curve to Cattewater Junction and the Yealmpton branch. It received a 45-lever frame in 1959, with the expansion of Laira yards. *Bernard Mills*.

Left: *Menheniot Signal Box* in Cornwall was an almost identical Type 5 design to that seen opposite at Teignmouth, albeit platform mounted. It opened in 1892, replacing an earlier box on the Down platform and by 1936 contained a 36-lever vertical tappet 3-bar frame. The box was decommissioned on 30 September 1973, and finally demolished in October 2007. It is recorded here in April 1973. *Terry Nichols*.

Below: *Plymouth Mill Bay Signal Box* photographed on 18 June 1966. The 58-feet wooden structure opened in 1914 with a 115-lever frame controlling the adjacent Millbay station and access to the docks complex. It closed on 14 December 1969 with the cessation of the remaining goods traffic. *Bernard Mills*.

Above: On 14 December 1963, Collett '2884' Class 2-8-0 No. 3863 trundles past the imposing *Exeter Middle Box*. Opened in July 1914, the 95-lever Type 31 structure controlled the eastern approaches to St David's station and the Red Cow level crossing. *Bernard Mills*.

Below: The 125-lever *Tiverton Junction Box* is captured during February 1975. Opened in 1932 following the quadrupling of the main lines through the station, the box also controlled access to the Tiverton and Culm Valley branches, closing in May 1986. *Terry Nichols*.

Right: The date is 8 September 1962 and the photographer is standing on the ex-Somerset and Dorset Railway platform at Highbridge, looking in the direction of Burnham-on-Sea. In this view all three of the station's signal boxes can be discerned, with closest to the right, the LSWR Type 4 *Highbridge 'A'*, which opened in 1895 and closed in 1914. Behind the bridge steps is the 1914 vintage GWR designed *Highbridge West*, which controlled the 'West of England' main line and became *Highbridge Crossing* from 1951. In the distance under the road bridge is the 1877 built *Highbridge 'B'*, which closed in June 1969 with the final rundown of the former S&D lines.
Douglas Twibell.

Below: The charming wayside station of Bishop's Nympton & Molland (on the Barnstaple branch) is seen on 3 October 1966. The 1937 built *Bishop's Nympton & Molland Signal Box* stands sentinel at the east end of the Down platform. Housing a 30-lever frame it closed with the branch in October 1966. As a footnote, the box nameboard sold at auction for £2000 in March 2021. *Bernard Mills.*

Dorchester West signal box was situated at the north end of the Down platform of the station of the same name, on the GWR Castle Cary to Weymouth route. Originally christened *Dorchester Signal Box* when opened in May 1908, it was renamed in 1949. It is a GWR Type 7B design and contained 29-levers. Control of the line passed to the BR(S) from February 1958, hence the green and cream paintwork adorning the box. By March 1968 the line was singled beyond here to Maiden Newton and control was passed to the nearby *Dorchester Junction* box, securing the fate of this structure.   *Bernard Mills*.

Above: The south-east elevation of *Westbury North Box* is seen in November 1975. Containing a 99-lever vertical tappet 5-bar frame, it was simply renamed *Westbury* in October 1978. Closure came in May 1984 with the opening of *Westbury Panel Box*. *Terry Nichols*.

Below: An overcast day in October 1967, finds a 'Brush Type 4' hauled express passing *Kennington Junction Signal Box* to the south of Oxford. Opened in 1901 with a 43-lever frame, it finally closed in December 1973 following demise of the Thame branch. *Doug Nicholls*.

Above: *Kidlington Signal Box* north of Oxford is captured across the adjacent allotment gardens in October 1968. As well as controlling the station and main line, the Type 5 box had responsibility for the Woodstock branch until its closure in 1954.   *Doug Nicholls*.

Below: Further north on the same line, we find *Heyford Signal Box* as it appeared in July 1967. Built in 1884 to a McKenzie & Holland design, it had 22-levers. The adjacent Brunel station building is currently being rebuilt at the Didcot Railway Centre.   *Doug Nicholls*.

WHERE DID THAT REFRESHMENT CAR COME FROM?
MICHAEL SEFI

It was during the currency of the BR(W) Summer 1955 Timetable that I first travelled on the Sundays ex-Taunton 5.10pm 'Refreshment Car' train to Paddington, joining at Savernake Low Level (LL) at 6.56pm. That train ran fast to London, with a set-down only call at Reading at 7.40pm, arriving at Paddington at 8.30pm.

At that time, we were staying for the summer in the village of Aldbourne, 7 miles from Hungerford but 15 miles from Savernake. So why were we driven to Savernake rather than Hungerford? Two reasons – the slow train, which had started from Trowbridge, did call at Hungerford at 7.22pm but didn't get to Paddington until 9.20pm (and had no catering facilities). But the main reason was the Refreshment Car on the Taunton train (with the bonus of the 8.30pm Paddington arrival), in which my father and I could have dinner.

During the Winter 1956-57 and the Summer 1957 Timetables I travelled regularly on that Sundays only train from Savernake LL, though not after Sunday 14 July. (It seems to be the case that Winter Timetable Sunday departures of the train from Taunton were usually at 4.45pm, and during the Summer period at 5.10pm). Nor did I travel on a Saturday, so avoided the problems so graphically demonstrated by *Summer Saturdays in the West* (David St. John Thomas & Simon Rocksborough Smith, David & Charles, 1973) which focused in the main on 27 July operations. After that I used that Sundays Taunton train from Savernake occasionally through until the summer of 1961.

I have identified a down working which may have provided the Refreshment Car and stock for the Taunton train. I've reviewed the detail in the Winter 1956-57 Timetable, (easier than in the Summer 1957 Timetable), so more on this analysis later, but I want to examine the origins of the stop at Savernake. And then review what happened to it after I stopped travelling on it.

It was in the Summer 1954 Timetable that a Sundays up train originating at Taunton and calling at Savernake LL first appears. I have very few of the regular timetable supplements so don't know if the Taunton 5.10pm with Refreshment Car, started with the Summer Timetable or a little earlier. But it is unlikely. It called at Frome and Westbury and had the same timing as described above at Savernake, Reading and arrival at Paddington.

A Weymouth Town departure at 4.10pm terminated at Westbury at 6.00pm; passengers off that train for Savernake, Reading and Paddington could join the 5.10pm ex Taunton (and get a meal) – while they had no means of getting to Pewsey and other stations before Savernake, (unless they were prepared to wait 90 minutes for a down train), they could nevertheless change at Savernake into the train originating at Trowbridge at 5.35pm, via Devizes, reaching Savernake LL at 6.44pm and departing from there at 7.03pm up the Berks & Hants line (all stations to Reading) and on to Paddington. It arrived in the up platform at Savernake as there was no connection from the up line into the branch bay.

This train then backed onto either the Marlborough down branch or the up refuge siding to allow the Taunton to overtake at 6.56pm – I can remember seeing it simmering, having backed out of the up line, while waiting to follow the Taunton. I think it must have been slightly alarming to passengers on the Trowbridge unfamiliar with the arrangement to find themselves going backwards, if indeed they did...!

But there is a bit of a mystery about this. In reviewing the signal box diagram for the Savernake West box, as published by G A Pryer in his *Signal Box Diagrams of the Great Western & Southern Railways Vol. 20*, there is a Wrong Direction (backing) signal (No. 8) at the country end of the up platform. I assume this was to allow a movement from that platform onto the down branch or possibly further back down the up into the up refuge siding; (the up siding is shown as having been taken out of use in 1955 and later lifted), or even further over onto the down line. However, the points (Nos. 14, 21 & 16) to enable those movements are shown in the Diagram without facing point locks and bars.

Left: On 27 August 1961, the 'Warship' hauled 4.45pm Taunton to Paddington express is seen approaching Savernake Low Level station. To the right, 'Hall' Class No. 5936 *Oakley Hall* stands at the head of the 5.35pm Trowbridge to Paddington service which had arrived at the station at 6.44pm. Having unloaded any passengers for Savernake, the complete train would then shunt back on to the Marlborough branch in order to clear the main line ready for the arrival of the faster train.

Above: Clearly with steam to spare, *Oakley Hall* waits impatiently to finally proceed eastwards with its London bound train. Whilst these images were captured on a Sunday, this unusual shunt manoeuvre was a regular feature at Savernake and could save passengers 'in the know' some 35 minutes by swapping trains. The MSWJ services ceased just two weeks later. *Transport Treasury*.

A 1959 photograph of the layout from the overbridge towards Savernake West box (*The Midland & South Western Junction Railway*, Jeffery Grayer, The Transport Treasury, 2022) shows several interesting features:

1. The up siding (off the up refuge siding and which ran behind the signal box) had indeed been removed with its associated points and signal (Nos.26 & 29).
2. The old style Wrong Direction signal at the country end of the up platform had been changed to a disc signal on a post.
3. The points at the country end of the up platform (No. 14) leading onto the (Marlborough) down branch clearly are not locked and there is no locking bar.
4. By 1959 the locking bar for the down main starting and branch signals (Nos.2 & 5) seems to have been removed.
5. The photograph seems to confirm the points to the up refuge siding off the up line are not locked, (No. 21), nor are the crossover points further back on the up line opposite the signal box (No.16).

To allow a passenger train (with passengers) to reverse from the up platform onto the branch without a facing point lock would be strictly forbidden, unless station staff were to get down onto track to padlock the points – and I never saw that happen. This was a regular movement over several years so it is difficult to believe that there was a special instruction permitting passengers to remain on the Trowbridge. So I can only assume that passengers on the Trowbridge for onward up destinations were required to disembark onto the Savernake up platform to allow the reversing movement

to take place, reboarding after the Taunton departed and the Trowbridge came back into the up platform. If any reader of this study has a copy of the BR(W) signalling diagrams for the two boxes at Savernake LL, I should very much appreciate a copy of them, or a copy of any instruction permitting the movement.

Why Savernake? What was so important about it that a fast train to Paddington had to call there, but not at places like Pewsey, Hungerford and Newbury? And at Reading to set down only? (Though by 1959 that restriction had been removed.) I suggest two reasons; the first is that Savernake LL was where the Marlborough branch trains met the Berks & Hants line. Marlborough was an important Wiltshire town, with a major public school, and while it had no direct services to London, it did have a good weekday service to and from Savernake to either the Low Level station or via the High Level station.

Admittedly there were only two on Sundays, neither into the Savernake LL bay platform in 1956/57, but through the High Level station. One of which allowed connection into the up Taunton. True, there would be a 35 minute wait, although prior to 1959 part of that time would be spent walking from the High Level station, around 250 yards. In 1959 the HL station was out of use and trains for Andover came down the branch into the up platform at the LL station and proceeded on their way to turn off the up line at Wolfhall Jct. In 1959 the LL connection was at 6.35pm – smart running necessary with the Trowbridge due at 6.44pm and the Taunton at 6.56pm!

And that is the second reason; Marlborough and Savernake High Level (HL) were on the old Midland and South Western Junction Railway which ran between Cheltenham Spa and Andover Junction – a dagger through the heart of the Great Western perhaps? Needless to say, after Grouping in 1923 the line came under the authority of Paddington. On Sundays in 1954 there were two trains a day, both to Andover and both calling at Savernake HL with the afternoon train calling as described. While there was no Sunday service between Cheltenham and Swindon Town, there were the two trains between there and Andover. What's more, the trains actually started from Swindon, so passengers from the Great Western main line, east and west, could reach Marlborough, for example, and perhaps as importantly could get to Chiseldon Camp Halt which even as late as 1954 was an important destination for the nearby military camp which had continued as such after the Second World War. (The camp had been a major depot during WW2, being used for the build-up of American forces prior to D-Day.)

Looking back from the introduction of that Sundays Taunton train in the summer of 1954, what of the Savernake LL call? The Winter 1953/54 Timetable shows that the 12.00pm ex Penzance called at Savernake LL at 6.55pm. That train had various stops in Cornwall and at Plymouth a Refreshment Car was either added or began service. From Plymouth it was non-stop to Exeter. From there it passed Taunton, but with calls at Frome and Westbury, and then there was the call at Savernake LL. From there it ran non-stop to Reading to set-down only, reaching Paddington at 8.30pm. The same trains described from Weymouth, Trowbridge and Swindon earlier in this study ran with their connections to much the same timings.

With minor changes to timings (although the Penzance departure was at 12.15pm) the Summer 1953 service was the same, but with the Refreshment Car operating from Penzance. The call at Savernake LL was as before at 6.55pm, but arrival at Paddington was 8.35pm.

A similar pattern is seen for Winter 1952/53 and Summer 1952. It seems to be the case that catering was from Penzance in the Summer period and from Plymouth during the currency of the Winter Timetable.

(Probably as a temporary measure so far as our train was concerned, the Restaurant Car service was suspended from 15 October 1951. Service was restored in the Summer 1952 Timetable, but now to be known as a 'Refreshment Car', previously Restaurant or Dining Car as in GWR days. These vehicles reverted to the original name 'Restaurant Car' in the 1957/58 Timetable.)

With minor timing changes, the pattern back to the first BR(W) Timetable, for Summer 1948, is much the same, though from the Winter 1950 Timetable the Reading call became set-down only – previously this restriction did not apply.

The last GWR Timetable, from October 1947, was much the same, the only significant timing change was that the Swindon-Andover train was somewhat earlier so that passengers had just over an hour to make their way from the High Level station to the Low Level station! I do not have timetables during the Second World War other than one from late September 1939; the previous pattern with a Sunday evening call at Savernake by a (reasonably) fast train is clear.

Going back pre-War to the summer of 1937, the equivalent Sunday Savernake call was by the 1.00pm ex Newquay, with Restaurant Car, calling at Par, Liskeard and Plymouth, departing from there at 3.00pm. It ran non-stop to Exeter, dep. 4.22pm, and from there non-stop to Savernake, departing at 6.10pm. It then ran non-stop to Paddington, arriving at 7.35pm. The Time Table note for passengers for Reading travelling on the Newquay train advised them to change at Savernake (and wait 47 minutes) to catch a slow up train originating at Trowbridge at 5.42pm which was due to arrive at Reading at 8.16 pm (and finally Paddington at 9.12pm).

On those summer 1937 Sundays at Savernake, there was one morning up slow, originating at Trowbridge at 7.00am, then nothing until the Newquay described above, followed by the Trowbridge and finally a somewhat speedier train originating at Weymouth Town at 5.25pm, calling at Savernake at 7.42pm with various calling points, arriving at Paddington at 9.20pm. This train even had a Buffet Car!

As to the Savernake connection, the afternoon train from Swindon Town departed there at 5.10pm, Marlborough at 5.41pm and arrived at Savernake High Level at 5.50pm, giving 20 minutes to get down to the Low Level station. From the Service Timetable for the summer of 1937, the train actually appears to have started from Cricklade, possibly with milk vans, at 4.40pm, arriving at Swindon Town at 4.55pm. To complete the detail, the make-up (consist) of the Newquay was two van thirds, two composites, four thirds and a 'dining car unit' (three coaches), plus a brake composite to be attached at Plymouth.

Looking back earlier than this, while an evening up fast calling at Savernake is a feature of Sunday timetables, its starting points were variously Paignton, Kingswear and Penzance, always with a 'Dining Car' (described as a 'Tea and Dining Car Train' in the Winter 1935/36 schedule). The connection from Swindon Town etc was via the High Level station, though, sometimes requiring a ten minute sprint from High Level to Low Level…! Some called at Reading, others were set-down only. The Summer 1932 train, from Kingswear, did call at stations to Newton Abbot, then Teignmouth and Dawlish, but from there was fast to Savernake, omitting Exeter, Taunton etc. The Penzance train in Winter 1927 started at 11.10am, but the Dining Car was only available from Exeter, and it had a call at Taunton. Reading was set-down only, with arrival at Paddington at 7.50pm.

When that Savernake call first began, I cannot say as I don't have a complete run of GWR Timetables, but it was the case that in the Summer 1927 Timetable the 12.25pm ex Penzance would only call at Savernake on notice being given at least three hours before what would be its 6.30pm call. Not only did that train not stop at Taunton, it also was non-stop through Reading, with arrival at Paddington at 7.55pm.

In 1922 and 1925 there was no up fast Sunday call and the only (non-catered) train was the ubiquitous Trowbridge up slow, calling at Savernake around 6.55pm, and arriving at Paddington around 9.20pm. Before the First World War this also seems to have been the regular pattern, but with some timing variances.

I mentioned earlier that after 1957 I caught that Sundays Savernake LL fast to Paddington occasionally until the summer of 1961 and the pattern of service was much as described for 1956/57. But in the Winter 1958/59 we find that the Swindon-Andover train was re-routed to the Low Level station, with the High Level station no longer in use. In the R A Cooke Track Layout Diagrams Section 22 the actual closure of the track through the High Level station is shown as taking place in June 1959.

There are other Sunday connection/timing changes before 1961, but none were of great significance to the Savernake to London passenger. It was in the winter of 1961 that the writing on the wall began to appear – the Taunton Restaurant Car was downgraded to a Buffet Car. But the major change was that the Swindon to Andover line had closed to passengers in September 1961 and there was no longer a Trowbridge train. Instead, a down train from Paddington (leaving at 4.15pm) terminated at Savernake at 6.21pm; I presume it ran onto the out of passenger use Marlborough branch. It started back to London at 7.20pm, arriving at Paddington at 9.18pm. Was this a diesel multiple unit?

Looking forward through to the winter of 1963, the pattern stayed much the same, with some timing changes, although the catering had reduced to the status of Miniature Buffet! But sadly, in the Summer 1964 Time Table, Savernake no longer had a Sunday service and the station closed finally on the 18 April 1966.

As to the Marlborough branch, it stayed open for freight until September 1964, and also for school specials in connection with the start and finish of terms at Marlborough College. (I can remember a similar situation when I was at boarding school in Somerset; school special trains ran from Paddington to Frome and, I think later, Westbury. Trunks were sent PLA [Passenger Luggage in Advance] to Chilcompton on the Somerset and Dorset, aka the Slow and Dirty, and brought from there to the school.)

To go back, now, to the Winter Timetable for 1956/57, a detailed exploration of train movements on Sundays and the preceding Saturday quickly reveals that there was an 11.15am Sundays train from Paddington, with a

The west end of Savernake Low Level, with a 0-6-0PT hauled train in the Marlborough branch bay platform. *Great Western Trust*.

Refreshment Car, going via Bristol and terminating in Taunton at 3.19pm. Shown in Table 61 (London, Reading, Didcot etc, Bristol and Taunton) it does not appear in Table 62 (London, Reading, Newbury etc, Weymouth and Taunton) surprisingly. I suggest that the stock (including the Refreshment Car) may have formed the 4.45pm starting in Taunton and calling at Savernake at 7.05pm having called at Frome and Westbury. (It also called at Lavington – the only up service of the day [there was no down service there on Sundays].) As before the Taunton was non-stop from Savernake to Reading to set-down only and it arrived in Paddington at the customary 8.30pm.

However, I am in some difficulty over this; having reviewed as best I can Refreshment Car trains starting from Paddington, I eliminated all trains likely to provide a Refreshment Car and stock to Taunton other than the 11.15am ex-Paddington described above. But in reviewing up services, there was a Taunton departure at 4.35pm having originated in Plymouth and Paignton. This train ran ahead of the 4.45pm described above, was non-stop from Taunton to Reading, set-down only, and on to Paddington, arriving at 7.20pm. The interesting point is that the train had a Refreshment Car, also from Taunton. As the train had an eight minute stop at Taunton, that could well have been time enough to attach the car, if that is what happened.

So I have an extra Refreshment Car at Taunton, source unknown – hence the title of this study! I have seen a photograph of around that time, running up to London, as ECS, consisting entirely of Refreshment Cars. Could one of those have been dropped off at Taunton? And what about staffing?

Unfortunately, I do not have Service timetables for the 1956/57 period. (I do have a complete set for June 1953, but those are no help in this case.) I assume the BR(W) had its equivalent of the GWR *Programme of Working of Coaches in Through Trains*, (a copy of which I do have for the summer of 1937 – a fascinating read!).

As to the 11.15am from Paddington, terminating in Taunton – it had a history prior to Summer 1954, but that's another story.

RILEY IN COLOUR: STILL WITH US

As can be seen from the inside cover advert to this issue, there are some exciting developments on the horizon relating to the R C Riley colour archive. As a taster of what is to come, we present a selection of his photographs featuring locomotives that survived the cutter's torch. No captions, just pure glorious colour!

THE GREAT WESTERN TRUST (GWT) - BULLETIN NO. 10

I am surely not alone in my delight of the article by Jim Horsnell 'Keeping the GWR on Track' in *WT* Issue No 10. The stories of the staff who were the vital but often ignored by history, key resource to such large companies and their own life story, is in my opinion of crucial importance if we are ever to try to truly understand and appreciate how working for such institutions was in reality. We can never adequately appreciate the world of ours that we take for granted today, if we haven't the reference for it given us by the stories of life spent years before. Without those folk, we would not be here today, in our own 'time bubble'.

All through Jim's article are items, examples of which we have in the Trust's Collection, all of which came to us from individuals such as Jim, or from their descendants who, more often than not, 'discovered' granddad's papers e.t.c. in a tatty box or suitcase in the loft, and wondered if it might be something the Trust would like to add to our archive. The more our Staff related section of the Collection grows, the more we know, the more of their stories are preserved for future generations, and of course, the happier I am!

Where to begin? Well in our Display Room we have tried to use its very modest space for an Office Scene. It is impossible to describe to visitors every item we have used to make it representative, but Jim's mention of ink and steel nib pens prompts me to say that we have numerous examples and that each and every steel nib was made for the GWR, and stamped with 'GWR' and the nib size. Yes there were many sizes and they were supplied in beautiful boxes! Even pencils were branded too, and to ensure each one was used to its utmost, we have sprung steel tubes by which when the pencil was too short to hold, they could slide over the short stub, to continue its use! Yes, those tubes were branded 'GWR' too!

Jim's attendance at the GWR's own Signalling Classes at Royal Oak reflects a very significant initiative which began way back in 1903 when the Signalling School was created deliberately and boldly for **all staff**, not just those in the S&T Department. The Trust holds a significant archive of that event and its consequences which could be a future WT Bulletin in itself. Crucially revolutionary at that time for the GWR, its advocates specifically announced it was to counter the prevalence of time served promotions over actual ability!

Jim mentions his father's early employ at Brentford Goods and his accident falling into a barge there. If you've wondered why the GWR, Brunel specifically, drove the GWR there in the first place, the use of Brentford Docks enabled them to avoid the heavier dock fees in London itself, for the massive importation of Permanent Way sleeper timbers.

Jim recalls staff privilege tickets. Here is yet another *WT* article if needed, on that regime, which in its earliest days the GWR was hardly an advocate of what became the Railway Employees Privilege Ticket Association (REPTA) and REPTA's history deserves its own day in the sun.

Jim also describes Jacob's Ladder bridge at West Ealing. Well by pure coincidence, our late founding Trustee, Fred Gray always reflected on his youthful train spotting there and an old chap who helped him as he had a telescope (maybe a retired sailor?) for identifying distant trains!

Jim was a member of the GWR Operatic Society and that organisation alone is a rich part of our Collection, not least quite recently we acquired the wonderful documents relating to its inception and the support given it by Sir Felix Pole.

I cannot exclude Jim's mention of the many staff outings. This aspect alone of our Staff related Collection, is full of such mementos, be it their programmes and photos, and that they were part of seemingly every GWR Department's staff, all however reflecting social class divisions! Much of the material effects of ex GWR and even BR(W) staff we are donated, include such outings, which today's employees can only wonder at.

As Jim closed his article sadly reflecting upon the wilful hand of Raymond in clearing Paddington Offices of 'GWR history', our long retired Trustee and Railway Historian, Philip Kelley had first-hand experience of its effect. Staff left 'items' in boxes in the corridors that miraculously disappeared overnight! We are certain that much of historic value that the Trust now holds, was once in those boxes, saved from oblivion by caring staff who knew better than Raymond that history would judge his attitude, short sighted at best, wanton at worst.

Thank you Jim, we are all the better for your contribution.

Peter Rance - GWT Trustee & Collection Manager.

THE GUARD'S COMPARTMENT

ISSUE 9

Dr Tony Stead wrote to address the question posed on **Page 75** about whether the 'Wallingford Station Box' sign survived. Arthur Isaac was appointed as clerk at the station soon after being demobilised from military service with a promise of promotion to Senior Clerk soon after, a position he held up until closure in 1965. Around the time of the branch line's demise, Arthur was able to purchase several Cholsey artefacts including the signal box's clock (he still holds the sales receipt for £1 10s 6d). He also bought the brass plates from the box's levers, and on final closure the signal arms and the cast iron sign 'WALLINGFORD STATION BOX'. After closure Arthur continued to work for BR at Head Office (Marylebone), commuting there daily from his new home near Ross-on-Wye. He kept all these items in his collection of railway artefacts until recently when he donated the sign and semaphore signals to Cholsey and Wallingford Railway (CWR), he also allowed us to copy numerous photos taken in and around the Station from the later years of operation. The photo shows these items laid out in front of him when the railway collected them from him. In the future the sign will, hopefully, once again adorn a signal box at the Wallingford terminal of the CWR.

--- o O o---

ISSUE 10

Andrew Royle expands upon the image of the Western Class on Hatton Bank on **Page 60.** One interesting point to make is that No. D1036 *Western Emperor* is ascending Hatton Bank on the slow line (normally only used by freight trains), thus suggesting this was a Sunday. 'Western' fans will tell you that Crewe-built D1036 was unique in having its numberplates mounted slightly higher up the cabside, which begs the question why? Did an employee at Crewe misread the instructions as to exactly where the plates should go? The loco appears to be immaculate so was probably only a matter of days into service, being new to traffic from Laira in August 1962. In the relatively short period that the Westerns worked the northern route to Birmingham and Wolverhampton, I believe that all 74 class members would have passed Hatton before their replacement by Brush Type 4s in 1964. From around 1973, as class 52s, they frequently came back again on Paddington to Birmingham New Street services but I don't think some of the earliest withdrawals made a second visit - unless anyone knows otherwise.

Fred Finney offered the following location and date information. Class '302' 0-6-0PT No. 306 on **Page 8** is at Oswestry shed. I think the location of No.654 on **Page 12** is Corwen. This loco was based there in January 1901 and again in May 1922. The shed had a similar 45ft turntable until 1900. In relation to the photo of Barry 'K' Class No. 193 on **Page 49**, other publications give a date of August 1924 and location as Barry shed.

--- o O o---

PREVIEW WESTERN TIMES ISSUE 12

Published April 2025

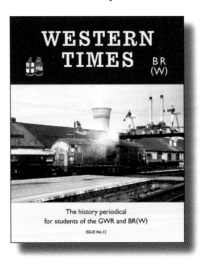

THE COMPLETE PIANO F
DUKE ELLINGTON

Arranged by Kenneth Baker

Wise Publications
London / New York / Paris / Sydney

MUSICROOM .COM

Exclusive Distributors:
Music Sales Limited
8 / 9 Frith Street,
London W1V 5TZ, England.
Music Sales Pty Limited
120 Rothschild Avenue,
Rosebery, NSW 2018,
Australia.

This book © Copyright 1992 by Wise Publications
Order No.AM90215
ISBN 0-7119-3274-3

Book design by Pearce Marchbank Studio
Compiled by Peter Evans
Music arranged by Kenneth Baker
Music processed by MSS Studios
Photograph courtesy of:
Redferns

Music Sales' complete catalogue lists thousands of titles and is
free from your local music shop, or direct from Music Sales Limited.
Please send a cheque / postal order for £1.50 for postage to:
Music Sales Limited, Newmarket Road, Bury St. Edmunds,
Suffolk IP33 3YB. 01234 714970

Your Guarantee of Quality
As publishers, we strive to produce every book to the
highest commercial standards.
The music has been freshly engraved and the book has been
carefully designed to minimise awkward page turns and to
make playing from it a real pleasure.
Particular care has been given to specifying acid-free,
neutral-sized paper which has not been chlorine bleached
but produced with special regard for the environment.
Throughout, the printing and binding have been planned to
ensure a sturdy, attractive publication which should give
years of enjoyment.
If your copy fails to meet our high standards, please
inform us and we will gladly replace it.

Unauthorised reproduction of any part of this publication by any
means including photocopying is an infringement of copyright.

Printed in the United Kingdom by
J.B. Offset Printers (Marks Tey) Limited, Marks Tey, Essex.

I GOT IT BAD AND THAT AIN'T GOOD

Words & Music by Paul Webster and Duke Ellington

© Copyright 1941 (renewed 1969) EMI-Robbins Catalog Incorporated, USA.
EMI-United Partnership Catalogue Limited, London WC2 for the UK & Eire.
All Rights Reserved. International Copyright Secured.

IT DON'T MEAN A THING
(IF IT AIN'T GOT THAT SWING)

Words by Irving Mills
Music by Duke Ellington

© Copyright 1932 by Mills Music Incorporated, USA. © Copyright Renewed 1960 Lawrence Wright Music Company Limited,
127 Charing Cross Road, London WC2 for all territories (except USA, Canada and Australasia).
All Rights Reserved. International Copyright Secured.

SOLITUDE

Words by Eddie de Lange & Irving Mills.
Music by Duke Ellington

In my sol - i - tude _____ you haunt me, with re - ver - ies _____ of days _ gone by.

In my sol - i - tude _____ you taunt me, with mem - or - ies _____ that nev - er die.

© Copyright 1934 Milsons Music Publishing Corporation, USA. Sole agents for the British Empire
(excluding Canada) and Europe J.R. Lafleur & Son Limited. Authorised for sale in the UK by
Permission of Boosey & Hawkes Music Publishers Limited, London.
All Rights Reserved. International Copyright Secured.

9

GO AWAY BLUES

Words & Music by Duke Ellington

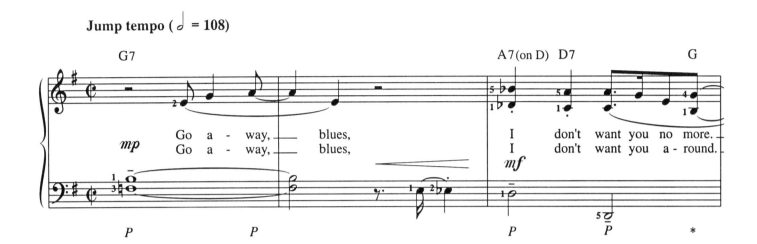

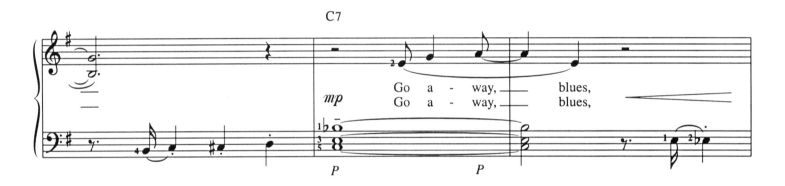

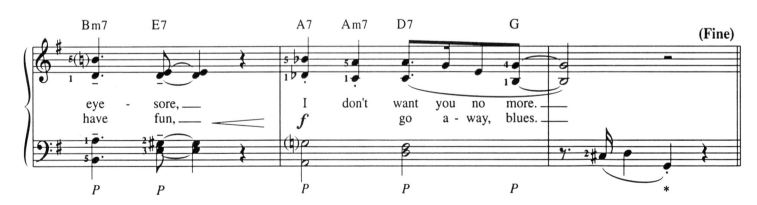

© Copyright 1944 Tempo Music Incorporated, USA. Campbell Connelly & Company Limited, 8/9 Frith Street, London W1.
All Rights Reserved. International Copyright Secured.

COME SUNDAY

By Duke Ellington

© Copyright 1966 Tempo Music Incorporated, USA. Campbell Connelly & Company Limited, 8/9 Frith Street, London W1.
All Rights Reserved. International Copyright Secured.

THE CREOLE LOVE CALL

By Duke Ellington

© Copyright 1928 Gotham Music Service Incorporated, USA. For British territories (excluding Canada and Australasia)
the property of Lawrence Wright Music Company Limited, 127 Charing Cross Road, London WC2.
All Rights Reserved. International Copyright Secured.

Coda

DO NOTHIN' TILL YOU HEAR FROM ME

Words & Music by Duke Ellington & Bob Russell

© Copyright 1943 EMI Robbins Catalog Incorporated, USA. EMI United Partnership, 127 Charing Cross Road, London WC2.
All Rights Reserved. International Copyright Secured.

oth- ers you've heard. ___ I have- n't a chance. ___ True, I've been

seen with some- one new, ___ but does that mean that I'm un- true? ___ When we're a-

part, ___ the words in my heart ___ re- veal how I feel ___ a- bout you. Some kiss may cloud my mem- o-

ry, and oth- er arms may hold a thrill. But please do no- thin' till you

hear it from me ___ and you ne- ver will.

PRELUDE TO A KISS

Words & Music by Duke Ellington, Irving Gordon & Irving Mills

© Copyright 1938 American Academy of Music Incorporated, USA. Authorised for sale
in the UK only by the permission of the sole agents, J.R. Lafleur and Son Limited.
All Rights Reserved. International Copyright Secured.

SATIN DOLL

Words by Johnny Mercer
Music by Duke Ellington & Billy Strayhorn

© Copyright 1953 & 1960 by Tempo Music Incorporated, USA.
Campbell Connelly & Company Limited, 8/9 Frith Street, London W1.
All Rights Reserved. International Copyright Secured.

I LET A SONG GO OUT OF MY HEART

Words & Music by Duke Ellington,
Irving Mills, Henry Nemo & John Redmond.

© Copyright 1938 Mills Music Incorporated, USA. © Copyright renewed 1966.
Lawrence Wright Music Company Limited, 127 Charing Cross Road, London WC2.
All Rights Reserved. International Copyright Secured.

I'M BEGINNING TO SEE THE LIGHT

Words & Music by Harry James,
Duke Ellington, Johnny Hodges & Don George

© Copyright 1944 Grand Music Corporation, USA. Campbell Connelly & Company Limited, 8/9 Frith Street, London W1.
All Rights Reserved. International Copyright Secured.

IN A SENTIMENTAL MOOD

Words & Music by Duke Ellington,
Irving Mills & Manny Kurtz

Romantically (♩ = 80)

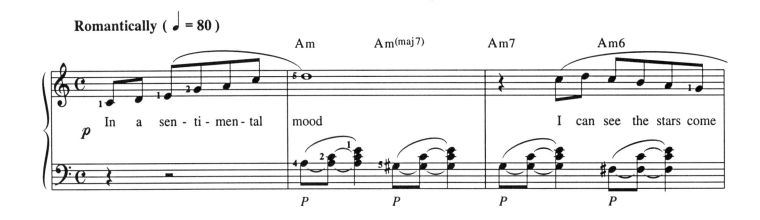

In a sen - ti - men - tal mood I can see the stars come

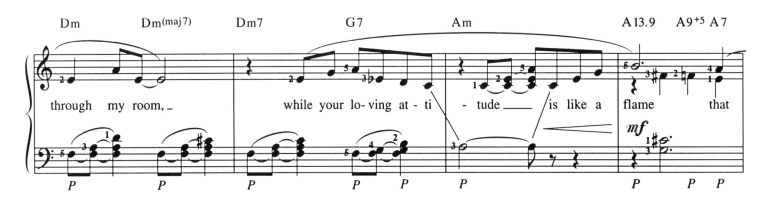

through my room, __ while your lo - ving at - ti - tude ____ is like a flame that

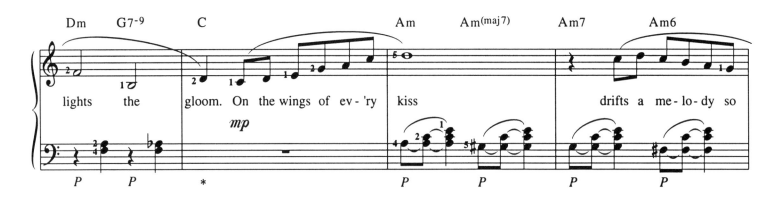

lights the gloom. On the wings of ev - 'ry kiss drifts a me - lo - dy so

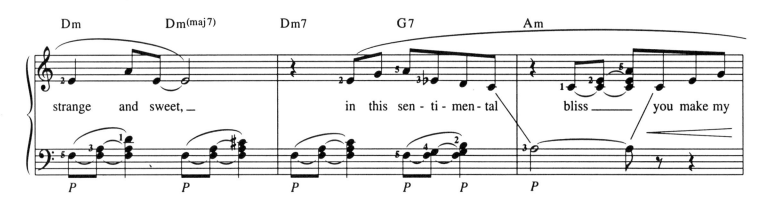

strange and sweet, __ in this sen - ti - men - tal bliss ____ you make my

© Copyright 1935 by American Academy of Music Incorporated, New York, USA. Republished containing new copyright matter 1935 by American
Academy of Music Incorporated. Sole agents for the British Empire (excluding Canada) and Europe, J.R. Lafleur and Son Limited.
Authorised for sale in Great Britain and Northern Ireland only by permission of Boosey & Hawkes Music Publishers Limited.
All Rights Reserved. International Copyright Secured.

DROP ME OFF IN HARLEM

Words by Nick Kenny
Music by Duke Ellington

© Copyright 1933 Mills Music Incorporated, USA. Campbell Connelly & Company Limited, 8/9 Frith Street, London W1.
All Rights Reserved. International Copyright Secured.

SOPHISTICATED LADY

Words by Irving Mills & Mitchell Parish
Music by Duke Ellington

© Copyright 1935 by Gotham Music Service Incorporated, USA. For Great Britain, Ireland and Colonies (excluding Canada & Australasia) the property of ATV Music, under license to MCA Music Limited, 77 Fulham Palace Road, London W6.
All Rights Reserved. International Copyright Secured.

CARAVAN

By Duke Ellington, Irving Mills & Juan Tizol

© Copyright 1937 American Academy of Music Incorporated, USA. Authorised for sale in the United Kingdom of Great Britain and Northern Ireland only by permission of the Sole Agent, J.R. Lafleur and Son Limited. All Rights Reserved. International Copyright Secured.

MOOD INDIGO

Words & Music by Duke Ellington,
Irving Mills & Albany Bigard

* This was the CHORUS in the original version

© Copyright 1931 by Gotham Music Service Incorporated, New York, USA. For Great Britain, Ireland and Colonies (excluding Canada and Australasia) the property of Lawrence Wright Music Company Limited, 127 Charing Cross Road, London WC2. All Rights Reserved. International Copyright Secured.

STOMP, LOOK, AND LISTEN

By Duke Ellington

© Copyright 1944 Tempo Music Incorporated, USA. Campbell Connelly & Company Limited, 8/9 Frith Street, London W1.
All Rights Reserved. International Copyright Secured.

PERDIDO

Music by Juan Tizol.
Words by Harry Lenk & Ervin Drake

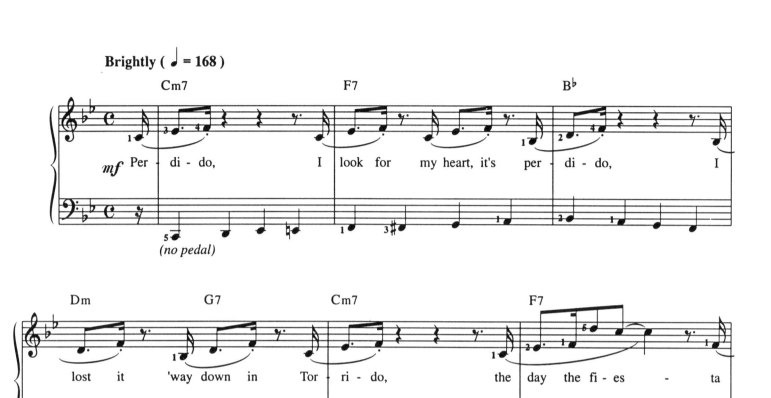

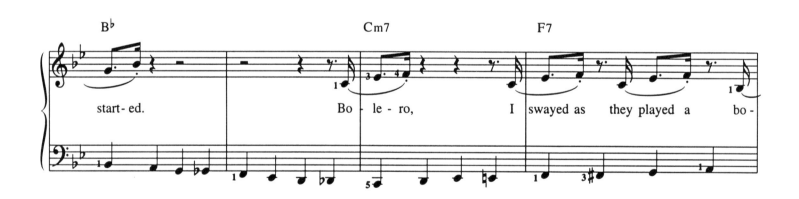

© Copyright 1942 Tempo Music Incorporated, USA. Campbell Connelly & Company Limited, 8/9 Frith Street, London W1.
All Rights Reserved. International Copyright Secured.

TIME'S A-WASTIN'

Words & Music by Duke Ellington,
Mercer Ellington & Don George

Groovin' (♩ = 108)

mf Lis-ten, ba-by, the time's a-wast - in', ___

an' I'm tell-in' ya, it's dis-grac - in', ___ Miss-in' Kis-ses we should be tast-

___ in', su-gar child, now I'm beg-gin' your lips to hast - en, ___ I

f need 'em so, ___ 'cause I got-ta feel-in' I got - ta glow.

© Copyright 1945 Burke and Van Heusen Incorporated, USA.
Campbell Connelly & Company Limited, 8/9 Frith Street, London W1.
All Rights Reserved. International Copyright Secured.

41

TAKE THE 'A' TRAIN

Words & Music by Billy Strayhorn

© Copyright 1941 Tempo Music Incorporated, USA. Campbell Connelly & Company Limited, 8/9 Frith Street, London W1.
All Rights Reserved. International Copyright Secured.

AIR CONDITIONED JUNGLE

By Duke Ellington

© Copyright 1950 Tempo Music Incorporated, USA. Campbell Connelly & Company Limited, 8/9 Frith Street, London W1.
All Rights Reserved. International Copyright Secured.